CAPITAL PUNISHMENT

CAPITAL PUNISHMENT

Lloyd R. Bailey

CONTEMPORARY
CHRISTIAN
CONCERNS
SERIES

JAMES M. EFIRD, EDITOR

ABINGDON PRESS
NASHVILLE

CAPITAL PUNISHMENT: WHAT THE BIBLE SAYS

Copyright © 1987 by Abingdon Press

This book is printed on acid-free paper.

Library of Congress Cataloging-in-Publication Data

Bailey, Lloyd R., 1936-
  Capital punishment.
  (Contemporary Christian concerns series)
  Bibliography: p.
  1. Capital punishment—Biblical teaching.
  I. Title. II. Series.
  BS680.C3B35   1987   261.8'3366   87-12557

ISBN 0-687-04626-2 (alk. paper)

MANUFACTURED BY THE PARTHENON PRESS AT
NASHVILLE, TENNESSEE, UNITED STATES OF AMERICA

* * *

Dedicated to my teachers, from church school to graduate program, who taught me to listen carefully to the Bible as the Word of God rather than seek to improve upon it by means of human values. They would have agreed with the ancient rabbis, "Do not seek to be more righteous than your Creator." (Eccl. Rab. 7.33)

CONTENTS

*T*here are literally thousands of persons in this country and over the world languishing in prison cells awaiting execution for crimes for which they have been convicted. In the United States, whenever one of these persons is actually scheduled to be put to death there is a renewal of the debate concerning the death penalty. Is it just? Is it fair? Does it deter? Is it "cruel and unusual punishment"? In these heated and emotional discussions, curiously enough, the Bible is quoted by defenders of each side of the debate.

Since the purpose of this series is to examine what the Bible actually does and does not say about contemporary concerns, it seemed appropriate to solicit a volume on the Bible and capital punishment. To this end I asked my distinguished colleague, Dr. Lloyd R. Bailey, Sr., to undertake this investigative task. This book is the result of his labor. Since the primary assignment of the writers for this series is to find out and present "what the Bible says," the volumes thus far have stimulated some lively exchanges. This volume will evoke the same response, perhaps more so.

Regarding highly emotional issues such as this, divine sanction is considered desirable for support for a particular position. Frequently, defenders of both positions will use biblical texts incorrectly in the attempt to enlist support for their views. It is one thing to be honest with a text and admit that one does not agree with it. It is altogether different to read one's preconceived ideas into the text so that one can then agree with it. The purpose of this series and this volume is to guard against imposing on the biblical texts ideas which they do not teach. Dr. Bailey has sought to present the biblical teachings about capital punishment against the backdrop of their own time and place and to present the rationale of the biblical writers and thinkers for their positions. I think that this volume can serve as a lively stimulus for further discussion of this issue, since the author has attempted to be perfectly honest about the biblical teaching.

That is what this series is about, and we are indebted to Dr. Bailey for this provocative volume.

JAMES M. EFIRD

My awareness of the problem to which the present volume is addressed came to me at an early age. A young man was being tried for murder in my home town during a summer of my grade school days. In the rural surroundings of this small town (Burnsville, North Carolina), court week provided the best entertainment available, and my father took me along to become acquainted with the proceedings.

The solicitor began by seeking to demonstrate that the accused had in fact committed the crime with which he was charged: murder, in violation of the criminal code of the state. Then, seeking to bolster the chances of conviction, he began to appeal to the religious faith of the jurors. He turned to the Ten Commandments and reminded them that "thou shalt not kill" (Exod. 20:13 KJV). Thus, he said, the defendant had broken not only the laws of man but also the laws of God, and so all the more he deserved to be put to death.

The defense attorney, aware of the power of this two-pronged attack upon his client's life, sought to reverse the thrust of the biblical injunction. He pointed out that, after all, execution was itself a form of killing. The commandment, then, should prevent the jurors (if they have religious sensitivity) from convicting the defendant of murder in the first degree. To do so would be a violation of the Bible! What the solicitor was doing, he suggested, was baldly asking the jurors to defy the Word of God!

Whether this reasonable argument, this seeming ambiguity of the biblical injunction, puzzled the jurors, I do not know. I do know that it puzzled me, and I have observed that it continues to confuse readers of the Bible to the present day. Thus, when North Carolina (and other states) resumed execution after a break of a decade or more (having awaited clarification of its legality by the U.S. Supreme Court), the Bible was invoked on both sides of the issue. The debate raged in letters to the editors of newspapers (both secular and ecclesiastical) and also in conversation between the students at my educational institution. Unfortunately, when the students asked me for assistance in clarifying the issue, there was little written material to which I could direct them, at least not much that was competent, clearly written, and readily available. Perhaps, then, the present volume will find some justification.

It may be useful, at the outset, to state what the goal of the present volume is and is not. It is not to state and defend, on biblical grounds, the author's personal opinion about whether modern governments should or should not authorize execution. It is not to argue, on pragmatic grounds based upon sociological findings, whether or not execution serves as a deterrent. It is not to determine whether execution is, as commonly stated, cruel and unusual punishment. It is not even to suggest to this or that religious group (denomination) what its stance should be on this particular issue. After all, there are a great variety of sources to which religious groups turn for ethical direction: not merely the Bible (Hebrew Bible, New Testament, Deuterocanonical books, i.e., Apocrypha), but also subsequent tradition (Talmud, Fathers of the church, the Protestant reformers), reason, experience, cultural values, and personal feelings. I realize, at the same time, that many theologians have suggested, rightly or wrongly, that Christian ethics need not be (or even cannot be) "biblical."

Rather, my goal is in keeping with the general title of the series to which this volume belongs: to investigate and present *what the Bible says*. I shall describe biblical mentality and practice as they relate to capital punishment during the period when the Bible was taking shape. I will seek to emphasize that which is central to the Bible's own agenda, and not pick and choose texts (as is often done) in order to support a preconceived notion. This will necessitate pointing out that certain passages in the Bible will not bear the weight that persons or groups have tried to place upon them. My overarching concern will be that the Bible be heard properly; that it not be abused in the service of other agendas when it is called upon to testify in the contemporary debate. (This is hardly a surprising goal for a professor of biblical studies, but it is one made necessary by such constant abuse of biblical texts.)

Anyone who undertakes a study of this topic will quickly be struck by its complexities. The issue becomes even more difficult when one goes beyond the descriptive task (what the text said to its own generation) to the issue of contemporary usage (what the text would mean now, were its authors with us). To the latter task I will turn but briefly toward the end, raising more questions than supplying answers. The issue is much more complex than many of those who discuss it would like to admit. As my colleague Stuart Henry is wont to say, "To fools, all things are simple!"

As this volume neared completion, an article appeared in the local newspaper (*Durham Morning Herald*, Aug. 29, 1986, p. 10-A) which indicates that the Bible and the courtroom still "mix." A defense attorney for a woman convicted of first-degree murder (for having burned her infant alive) had argued against that potential verdict by citing Matthew 25:40: "As you did it to . . . the least of these my brethren, you did it to me." (To be precise, his argument was not against the death penalty per se, but that his client, a diagnosed schizophrenic, was one of "the least of us.")

Gratitude is hereby expressed to my M.Div. student Timothy J. Rogers for the paper entitled "Biblical Perspectives on Capital Punishment," which he prepared under my direction during the fall semester of 1984.

The Practice

*T*hat capital punishment was sanctioned by the society out of which the Hebrew Bible ("Old Testament") grew, indeed that it is mentioned with some frequency in the text, even the most casual reader should know. Such readers are likely to be less clear, however, about details of the practice. For what offenses was it mandated? By what methods was it applied? What groups or officials were authorized to pass sentence and carry it out?

Such factual data will be our point of departure. In chapter 2, we will turn to the deeper issue of the rationale (justification, goals) of the practice.

Capital Offenses

At first glance, the number of crimes for which the death penalty was considered justified by ancient Israel's canonical thinkers may seem quite large to some modern Western readers. This is because, in the present century, the number of such offenses has been drastically reduced. In eighteenth-century England, by contrast, there were 160 separate offenses for which one might be put to death.

The nature of certain of the offenses may also be surprising to the modern reader and in some cases seem frivolous. Murder and kidnapping perhaps we can understand: They threaten the security of the reader, and it is in our "enlightened self-interest" to oppose them as strenuously as possible. So goes the modern rationale. But cursing one's parents, sorcery, and sacrifice to foreign gods? These may strike the modern reader sequentially as petty, superstitious, and religiously narrow.

To explain the danger which was seen in each of the capital offenses would take a volume within itself, and this is not the task of the present one. It is sufficient for our purposes to realize that this punishment was proposed within a theological framework. That is, it was handed down and accepted as the will of God, revealed under the most sacred and explicit of circumstances.

The attached list of seventeen offenses is limited to those stated in the Pentateuch (the *torah* of Moses—the books of Genesis, Exodus, Leviticus, Numbers, and Deuteronomy), and is not necessarily complete. These offenses are prohibited by God through the agency of Moses. Still other offenses were punishable by death during the monarchical period (which began several centuries after Moses and extended to the exile of the Judeans to Babylonia, i.e., 1020–587 B.C.E.). King Solomon, for example, orders the execution of his older half-brother Adonijah for an act which he considers treasonable (I Kings 2:13-25). Such an act may have found theological justification (rather than raw power and the survival of the fittest) in the biblical claim of an eternal covenant with David and his descendants (II Sam. 7). However, since the role of the king in the administration of justice has been much debated (Boecker, chapter 1), since the date (and earliest form) of the Davidic Covenant is uncertain, since it is difficult to disentangle personal and theological motives in royal decrees and policies, and since only the Pentateuch has been accepted as Scripture by the totality of Israel, I have listed only those offenses which have traditional Mosaic authority. (The Sadducees and Samaritans, for example, rejected even the rest of the Hebrew Bible as Scripture.)

Capital Offenses	*Trial or Punishment*

The list is not necessarily complete, nor has every relevant citation been given for a particular offense. It is important to note that the verb generally used (a form of *m-w-t*, "to die") is not the same as that used in the sixth of the Ten Commandments, traditionally translated as "Thou shalt not kill." Each quotation is from the first source cited.

Few instances are to be found in the so-called "historical books" (Joshua–Esther in the RSV), because their focus is upon national destiny and monarchical leadership rather than upon activity in the local courts.

1. Murder (Exod. 21:12; Lev. 24:17):
"Whoever strikes a man so that he dies *shall be put to death*" (*môt yûmat*).

II Sam. 3:27; 4:5-12; 14:6-7; 21:1-9

2. Contempt for parents (Exod. 21:15, 17; Lev. 20:9):
"Whoever strikes his father or his mother *shall be put to death*" (*môt yûmat*).

"Whoever curses his father or his mother *shall be put to death*" (*môt yûmat*).

3. Trespass upon sacred areas or things (Exod. 19:12-13; Num. 1:51; 18:7):
"Whoever touches the mountain *shall be put to death*" (*môt yûmat*).

Acts 21:27-31

4. Kidnapping for ransom (Exod. 21:16; Deut. 24:7):
"Whoever steals a man,

whether he sells him or is
found in possession of him,
shall be put to death" (môt yûmat).

5. Sorcery (Exod. 22:18; Lev.
20:27):
"You shall not permit a sor-
ceress to live." (Lev. uses *môt
yûmat.)*

I Sam. 28:3, 9

6. Bestiality (Exod. 22:19;
Lev. 20:15-16):
"Whoever lies with a beast
*shall be put to death." (Lev. uses
môt yumât.)*

7. Sacrifice to foreign gods
(Exod. 22:20; 20:1-5; Deut.
13:1-19):
"Whoever sacrifices to any
god, save to the Lord only,
shall be utterly destroyed"
(yochoram).

Num. 25:1-9; II Kings
10:18-27

8. Profaning the Sabbath
(Exod. 31:14):
"Everyone who profanes it
shall be put to death" (môt yûmat).

Num. 15:32-36

9. Adultery (Lev. 20:10;
Deut. 22:22-24):
"If a man commits adultery
with the wife of his neighbor,
both . . . *shall be put to death"
(môt yûmat).*

John 8:3-11

10. Incest (Lev. 20:11-13):
"The man who lies with [vari-
ous relatives specified]
. . . *they shall be put to death"
(môt yumetu).*

11. Homosexuality
(Lev. 20:13):
"If a man lies with a male
. . . *they shall be put to death*"
(môt yumetu).

12. Blaspheming the Holy
Name (Lev. 24:16):
"He who blasphemes the
name of the Lord *shall be put to
death" (môt yûmat).*

Lev. 24:10-16; I Kings 21:10;
Acts 6:11; 7:58; 26:9-11

13. Contempt for certain judicial decisions (Deut. 17:8-
13):
"The man who acts presumptuously, by not obeying
. . . shall die [*mēt*]; so you shall
purge the evil."

14. False witness in court
against someone charged with
murder (Deut. 19:16-21):
"You shall do to him as he had
meant to do to his brother; so
you shall purge the evil from
the midst of you . . . life for
life."

15. Harlotry under specified
conditions (Lev. 21:9; Deut.
22:13-21):
"The daughter of any priest;
if she profanes herself by
playing the harlot . . . she
shall be burned with fire."

"They . . . shall stone her
to death . . . [for] playing the
harlot in her father's house."

Gen. 38:24

16. Negligence that results in
a death (Exod. 21:28-29;

Deut. 22:8):
"When an ox gores a man
. . . to death . . . and its
owner has been [previously]
warned . . . its owner . . . *shall
be put to death" (yûmat).*

17. False prophecy (Deut.
18:20):
"The prophet who presumes
to speak a word in my name
which I have not commanded
him to speak . . . *shall die"
(mēt).* (The verb will allow
death by divine decree, but
compare no. 13.)

Jer. 26:1-9 This may be a
case of sedition under royal
law; note, however, that he is
acquitted because he "spoke
in the name of the Lord" (v.
16).

The careful reader of Israel's legal materials will be struck
by their diversity in form, language, and content, as well as by
the fact that some of the Bible's major characters violate its
prohibitions seemingly with impunity. Those who wish to
understand the reasons for these curiosities may pursue the
matter with the aid of Appendix A.

Methods of Execution

Although there is no systematic discussion of the topic in
the Bible, a survey of the accounts of execution reveals that
the accepted methods were stoning, burning, and the use of
various weapons of war (sword, arrow, etc.).

The most common means apparently was stoning; the
reason for this will appear below. It is specified for the
following offenses: contempt for parents (Deut. 21:21),
trespass upon sacred areas (Exod. 19:13), sorcery (Lev.
20:27), worship of foreign gods (Deut. 17:5), profaning the
Sabbath (Num. 15:35), adultery (Deut. 22:22), blasphemy
(Lev. 24:14), and harlotry (Deut. 22:21). In addition, stoning
is attested in cases of violation of *herem* (a pronouncement by

which objects obtained through a "holy war" are to be destroyed—to keep them is tantamount to theft of God's property; see, e.g., Josh. 7:25). It also seems to have been popular with mobs, comparable to a modern "lynch mob," who rebelled against authority or who were enraged at some violation (Exod. 17:4; Num. 14:10). In one case (trepass upon sacred areas), shooting with arrows is an allowable alternative to stoning (Exod. 19:13).

Death by burning is specified in case of certain sexual offenses: marriage to one's mother-in-law (Lev. 20:14) and harlotry by a priest's daughter (Lev. 21:9). In another case, it is mentioned in connection with harlotry (Gen. 38:24) but the issue is a special one, complicated by the levirate regulation.

In cases where very large groups were to be put to death, usually for apostasy (worship of other gods), it seemed expedient to use the sword (Exod. 32:15-29). This was even mandated in the case of an entire city (Deut. 13:12-15). Indeed, apostate individuals (priests) are dispatched in this fashion (II Kings 23:20). Execution at the command of the king seems to have taken the form of beheading (II Kings 6:31; see also II Sam. 16:9).

As for murderers, they are to be struck down by the "avenger of blood" (Num. 35), presumably by whatever weapon is at hand, usually the sword. In that fashion, the ancient requirement of Genesis 9:6 would be satisfied: "Whoever sheds the blood of man, by man shall his blood be shed."

In contrast to the New Testament and the rabbinic period (where stoning was specified as the most severe of the options for execution), death by bloodshed seems to have been the ultimate horror in ancient Israel. It was, by then, possibly an irrational fear, grounded in previous (pre-Yahwistic) demonology: The demons lurking beneath the ground would be able to consume the blood (life-force) of the slain. Thus, Abel's blood "cries out from the ground" (Gen. 4:10). In Israel's canonical, Yahwistic thought, demons do not exist. Nonetheless, a fear of bloodshed, originally connected with demon worship, lingers after Israel's concept of the Deity has denied the power of demons and called their very being into question.

Specification of the Executioner

By what institution (institutions) were guilt and innocence decided, and at whose hand was a sentence of death to be carried out? Since the period of the Hebrew Bible covers some two thousand years, it is hardly surprising to find that new regulations and institutions sometimes arose without necessarily replacing the old ones. Thus, we need not expect comprehensive codes and absolute uniformity of legal practice. At the same time, it must be realized that the texts that have come down to us are not concerned to convey a systematic picture of legal procedure. The concern, rather, is to describe God's activity and Israel's response. Consequently, any modern description of the legal system must be gathered from scattered remarks made in passing in the texts.

Since one component of Israel's history involved a semi-nomadic way of life (e.g., the period of the patriarchs), where the head of the family (paterfamilias) had unrestricted authority over its members, we need not be surprised to find a story such as is related in Genesis 38: The patriarch Judah is able to pronounce a death sentence on his daughter-in-law without consultation of anyone. Another illustration may be found in Genesis 16: Abraham, as head of the family, is petitioned by Sarah that justice be done. It is an issue over which he has absolute jurisdiction. With the passage of time, however, restrictions were placed upon this so-called "father law."

In addition to the father, judicial authority is invested in the elders. The institution of the elders seems to have arisen from tribal law: Disputes between blood-related families were decided by an assembly of heads of families. This then gave rise to a formal legal assembly within settled village life.

The elders met in the public area of the city gate, and in some cases the paterfamilias' rights were surrendered to them. Thus, by the time of the Deuteronomic legislation, parents of contemptuous offspring were required to bring the rebel before the elders of the town. Nonetheless, the parents' testimony alone was sufficient to convict them, and "all the men of the town" were required to carry out the death sentence, which almost necessitated that it be by stoning (Deut. 21:18-21; see also 22:21).

Community-wide participation in execution is recorded in the case of the Sabbath violater (Num. 15:35-36), a blasphemer of the Holy Name (Lev. 24:14), trespass upon sacred areas (Acts 21:30-31), and adultery (John 8:3-11). Thus, it seems to have been the norm for the capital offenses which the Pentateuch specifies. Eyewitnesses to such crimes, who testified to what they had seen, were compelled to participate in, and indeed to initiate, the process of execution (Deut. 17:7), thereby impressing upon them the consequences of false witness. In certain other punishments, however, it is the elders themselves who carry out the sentence (Deut. 22:18-19).

That priests played a role in some judicial events is well attested. For example, when a case could not be decided on the basis of proof, the accused could seek to clear himself by means of oath or ordeal. The former consisted of a self-curse in case of false witness ("May God do so-and-so to me, if . . . "), and is alluded to in Exodus 22:8, 11. It was assumed that the fear of God was sufficient to ensure the integrity of the procedure, and thus the oath settled the matter (22:11). That the oath was to be taken in the presence of the priest ("near to God") is explicitly stated. In the ordeal the accused was subjected to a physical test administered by a priest, a procedure well attested throughout the ancient world. Since Numbers 5:11-31 contains a detailed and clear illustration, the reader is referred to it for clarification. (For further discussion, see Frymer.)

In matters of proper ritual ("the clean and the unclean"), the priests were the sole authority (Lev. 10:10), and by the time of Deuteronomy it is stated that they might play a role in "every dispute and every assault" (21:5) and in a process of appeal (17:8-13). We have no concrete example of how appeal took place, however. What is stated is that anyone who rejects the decision of the priest in matters of appeal is to be put to death (17:12). Rejection, at that stage, was apparently regarded as an uncompromising rejection of the covenant and of the Deity who undergirded it.

A separate judicial system arose under the monarchy. (The jurisdiction of such courts has been variously interpreted by modern scholars; see Boecker, pp. 40-49.) It is clear that soldiers and members of the royal bureaucracy were answerable to the king and could be executed at his command for violation of certain regulations (see II Sam. 19:16-23). It has been argued that ordinary citizens of the royal capitals (Samaria and Jerusalem) were subject to the jurisdiction of the king (as paterfamilias of the city?) in a way that citizens of other locations were not (see especially I Kings 3:16-27). It is also recorded that a king might appoint judges in the various cities of his realm (II Chron. 19:5). However, any attempt to infringe upon the jurisdiction of the local courts (elders) or of the "Judge" (who interpreted Israel's covenant with God; see I Sam. 7:15-17) was strenuously resisted. For example, see I Samuel 15, where King Saul's departure from Samuel's directive leads to a scathing denunciation. Nonetheless, the right of the king to set certain regulations for his subjects, and to execute those who violated them, was ordinarily not challenged. Indeed, the office was underwritten by Mosaic authority (Deut. 17:14-20), and one was instructed "not [to] revile God, nor curse a ruler of your people" (Exod. 22:28). It is a theological perspective on government that will be reiterated in the New Testament, as we shall see.

When it was necessary for one of the king's subjects to be executed, it was done by professional soldiers. The sword seems to have been the weapon of choice (II Sam. 4:12; I Kings 2:25).

What was the procedure in case of murder? In much Near Eastern thought, ancient and modern, the killing of a member of one's family or clan (extended family) by an outsider necessitated blood revenge. The blood of the kinsman must be avenged by the death of the killer. The apparent reason for this was that the clan had suffered a loss of its collective power as well as dishonor to its members. The prior balance between two groups had been upset and thus the killer's clan must suffer equal damage through blood vengeance (Boecker, pp. 36-38). Although modern Western persons, steeped in individualism, no longer share such deep-rooted feelings of solidarity, they may nonetheless be able to understand the pragmatic value of the custom. At a time when there was no central, wide-ranging administration of justice, it helped to ensure the safety of the individual and thereby to maintain the stability of the clan.

This ancient custom is apparently attested in the song of Lamech:

> I have slain a man for wounding me,
>   a young man for striking me.
> If Cain is avenged sevenfold,
>   truly Lamech seventy-sevenfold.
>   (Gen. 4:23-24)

An illustrative incident may be found in II Samuel 21:1-9, where the Gibeonites are granted the lives of seven of Saul's sons because of blood guilt resulting from his previous acts.

Israel sought to modify this ancient custom in at least the following three significant ways:

1. Killing was placed within a theological (rather than sociological and political) framework. Life belongs to God and thus cannot be taken merely to suit such human values as balance of power or pride of group (chapter 2). Therefore,

punishment must also be applied to the members of one's own group in case of murder (II Sam. 14:1-11).

2. Inability to apprehend the killer does not justify extending the blood vengeance to relatives: "Every man shall be put to death for his own sin" (Deut. 24:16).

3. A distinction must be made between justifiable killing and murder. Hence when Asahel was killed by the butt of Abner's spear after Abner had sought to avoid injuring him (II Sam. 2:18-23) and brother Joab avenged his death by killing Abner (3:26-27), it was nonetheless reckoned as an act of murder on Joab's part (I Kings 2:28-34). Similarly, "cities of refuge" were established throughout the country to which "manslayers" could flee from "avengers" (Num. 35:9-28). Should they be able to reach the city before the "avenger" overtook them, then they were immune until the elders of the city had reached a decision about whether they had acted intentionally. If the elders' decision was that they had so acted, then "the avenger of blood shall himself put the murderer to death." If not, then they were granted sanctuary in the city of refuge. However, should they stray outside the city, then their "avengers" could strike them down with impunity.

Whose obligation was it to assume the role of the "avenger" (go⁻el)? In other legal situations, the term is used for a near relative (hence RSV at Lev. 25:25, "next of kin"). Hence Boaz is the go⁻el for Naomi and Ruth (Ruth 2:20; 3:12), who acts to preserve the property of Ruth's husband (4:1-6). It is plausibly and generally assumed, therefore, that the "avenger" is a male relative of the slain. However, a few interpreters have suggested that he was a public officer sent out by the elders of the killer's city (Phillips, pp. 101-9).

Limitations and Safeguards

Unlike the codes of its neighbors (and unlike those of modern societies, for that matter), ancient Israel's Pentateuchal laws allowed capital punishment only for crimes against

God and against persons. Its ultimate concerns were the sanctity of life (chapter 2) and the purity of God's people and their worship. This conspicuously excludes, for example, execution for crimes against property (e.g., theft, burglary, arson). A burglar may not be killed during daylight hours (under the assumption that his agenda is theft?), but at night may be killed with impunity ("there shall be no bloodguilt for him," Exod. 22:2, the assumption being that the homeowner may justifiably expect violence?). It is a different matter, of course, with theft of God's property (e.g., items placed under *herem* in "holy wars," as in Josh. 7). That results in execution.

No exception is to be assumed in the case of David's reaction to the reported theft of a poor man's lamb (II Sam. 12:1-6): "The man who has done this deserves to die." That is impassioned rhetoric, with the thief's legal accountability then outlined: "He shall restore the lamb fourfold," in keeping with Exodus 22:1.

The capital crimes are often circumscribed with precise definitions and limiting circumstances. For example, it must be premeditated murder, and not accidental or out of necessity (Deut. 19:1-13). Contemptuous offspring must be clearly intransigent rather than occasionally annoying, and both parents must so affirm (Deut. 21:18-21). (It is doubtful that this meant a child, as opposed to grown offspring.) Sabbath-breaking is given an illustrative definition (Num. 15:32-36). The punishment for false witness is only in accordance with the damage it might have done (Deut. 19:19). Harlotry merits death only in cases of a woman yet in her father's house or the daughter of a priest (Deut. 22:21; Lev. 21:9). Judges must be aware that witnesses may be malicious or self-serving, and thus two witnesses are necessary for conviction. This is specifically stated for the charges of worship of foreign gods (Deut. 17:6) and murder (Num. 35:30), and possibly was the rule for the other capital cases as well. In order to prevent false witness, such persons must actually initiate the process of execution (Deut. 17:7).

There is evident concern that the death penalty be applied equitably. Whereas in other legal systems in the ancient Near East, monetary compensation was allowed in case of murder (Middle Assyrian Code, A.10; Hittite Laws, 1–5), in Israel it was strictly forbidden (Num. 35:31). Whereas such systems allowed a sliding scale of compensation according to the social status of the parties involved in a personal injury case (Hammurabi Code), the Bible arguably imposes the death penalty for killing even a slave ("he shall be punished," Exod. 21:20, according to the Samaritan Pentateuch, Talmud, and traditional Jewish interpreters). Thus, the well-to-do are forbidden legal advantage over their fellow citizens, in contrast to modern American society, where such advantage is easily available to the affluent.

It has been argued that, in some cases, the death penalty was the maximum of several options available in judicial decision (Wenham, p. 285). However, while there are a few cases that perhaps evidence uncertainty as to the gravity of the offense (blasphemy, Lev. 24:10-16; Sabbath violation, Num. 15:32-36), this is a slender basis for suggesting that "the penalties prescribed in the law were the maximum penalties."

A few scholars have argued, on grammatical grounds, that the sentence "shall be put to death" *(môt yûmat)* may indicate permission rather than demand, that is, it could mean, "may be put to death" (Buss, pp. 55-56). However, while such a translation of the phrase is grammatically possible, the contexts in which it occurs make it extremely unlikely (see Appendix B).

CHAPTER II

The Rationale

Since the Bible's legal sections are a subordinate part of its larger narrative purpose, they are not intended to be comprehensive. It is thus not surprising that such sections are scattered, fragmentary, incomplete, and that they lack a preface which sets out their justification and goals. In only a few instances will a motive for the death penalty be stated, and sometimes it is not necessarily the one that is at the heart of the matter. Nonetheless, there is an overall theological perspective at work.

Let us begin with the issue of deterrence, much under attack by sociologists and theologians in the present. The Deuteronomic legislation will categorically state from time to time that execution in Israelite society will have the following effect: "And all the people shall hear, and fear, and not act presumptuously again" (Deut. 17:13; see also 13:11; 19:20; 21:21). Ryrie (p. 217) may have had this in mind, although he cites only New Testament texts (II Pet. 2:13), when he states: "What, after all, is the purpose of capital punishment? . . . ultimately the biblical purpose seems to be the promotion of justice by civil government."

On a recent national news program ("Sixty Minutes"), a prosecutor was asked about his justification for trying a juvenile for murder (a particularly vicious instance of it, to be sure), and his heartfelt response was, "In order to send a message!" Opponents of the death penalty never tire of pointing out that, in their opinion and according to studies, the "message" is not clear; the deterrent fails to deter. In the case of those who subsequently commit the crime, the opponents are undeniably right. In principle, however, this does not bear upon the matter of whether it has prevented others from taking human life. There are those who will testify that it has. And so the discussion goes.

Deuteronomy clearly affirms that, for the society of its time, the punishment was an effective deterrent. It is a claim, undergirded with canonical authority, for which no counter-evidence is possible. Whether it continues to deter in our society (which the text does not state) is an issue that need not detain us here, despite all the passion that it has generated. And the reason is simply this: Deterrence is at the periphery of the Deuteronomist's concern (and of the entire Bible, for that matter). Whatever bonus effect it may have had (or does have), it does not touch upon the center of the Bible's attitude toward capital punishment. That center has to do with theology (as we will soon see), and it is a serious misunderstanding so to construe it that modern social sciences can pass judgment upon it. Canon, in such a case, has been reduced to evidence of an antiquated penology.

We move toward a more basic concept when we read another expression of the Deuteronomic legislation. Through the process of execution, "You shall purge the evil from the midst of you" (Deut. 13:5; 17:7; 19:13; 21:21; 24:7). (RSV's "purge," for the Hebrew verb *b-ʿ-r*, is rendered as "banish" in JB and "rid yourself of" in NEB.) It would be easy to suppose that the "evil" which is to be removed is the criminal, or even the repetition of the crime (i.e., that deterrence is again meant). That this is not the intention is suggested by Deuteronomy 21:1-9, where the corpse of a murder victim has been found and there is no way of knowing who committed the crime. The community must now enact a complex ritual wherein the Deity is implored to "set not the guilt of innocent blood in the midst of thy people Israel; but let the guilt of blood be forgiven them." Thereby "you shall purge the guilt of innocent blood from your midst."

The idea seems to be that the grave crimes for which "purging" is necessary are offenses in the eyes of the Deity, offenses which have inevitable negative consequences ("evil") for society. In case of murder, the Deity is offended and imputes bloodguilt to the group within which the event has taken place. The Deity then allows for a redeeming response on the part of the group, and if none is forthcoming, enacts justice in a way that only a Deity can.

While society-wide accountability for individual acts of violence may be alien to our modern Western mentality, with its emphasis upon individuality and freedom of the will, this basic conviction of the Bible remains clear and understandable; the Deity is deeply offended by certain acts and expects Israelites not only to avoid them but also to take appropriate action when anyone performs them.

The Deity's concern that certain actions not be tolerated is clarified when Israelite law is viewed in its overall theological context. Its starting-point is not such modern, rational, and pragmatic principles as "the greatest good for the greatest number," "enlightened self-interest," "personal freedom," or "public order." Rather, it is a religious law. As such, it goes beyond other ancient Near Eastern codes which invoke the gods of the society as their guarantors. King Hammurabi of Babylon, for example, in the prologue to his famous code, states that the great gods appointed him "to promote the welfare of the people . . . to cause justice to prevail in the land," and that Marduk had commissioned him "to guide the people aright, to direct the land." In the epilogue he continues, "By the order of Shamash, the great judge of heaven and earth, may my justice prevail in the land." The biblical perception, by contrast and comparison, is that God is more than a guarantor of the covenant (of which legislation is a part): God is a party to the agreement (covenant) which is articulated, as it were, in divine language.

Israel believed that the Deity (Yahweh; in English versions, "the Lord") had singled them out for no discernible reasons other than divine freedom and graciousness (Exod. 3:14; 33:19). Consequences of the selection (election) included: the promise of land, offspring, and blessing (Gen. 12:1-3); deliverance from Egyptian bondage (Exod. 3:6, 16-17); guidance through the Sinai wilderness (Exod. 13:21-22); the gift of the land of Canaan (Num. 13:1-2); and revelation of a body of regulations whereby (if the people responded in gratitude to the divine initiative) Israel would become "to me a kingdom of priests and a holy nation" (Exod. 19:6).

Israel's way of expressing this conviction resembles the treaties (covenants) which ancient Near Eastern monarchs made with their subordinates. The great king (God) has performed gracious deeds and now invites the recipient small state (Israel) to formalize a relationship and to respond in specified ways: (1) exclusive loyalty to the great king, and (2) consideration for the right of fellow covenant-members. Thus we read, at Exodus 20: "I am the Lord your God, who brought you out of the land of Egypt. . . . [therefore] You shall have no other gods before me. . . . Remember . . . You shall not."

From this understanding of the relationship between the Deity and Israel flowed the central motivation for obedience to the commandments: gratitude, perhaps best expressed by Jesus' words, "If you love me, you will keep my commandments" (John 14:15).

By similar analogy with political treaties, there was an expectation of blessing or curse upon those who, having freely accepted God's invitation, then either kept their word or betrayed it. There was a need to safeguard the covenant relationship from crimes against the Sovereign One (e.g., apostasy, profaning the Sabbath, blasphemy), from attitudes which destroy the People of God (e.g., sorcery, adultery, false witness), or from acts which tarnish the holiness which is to characterize this "realm of priests" (e.g., bestiality, harlotry, incest).

Prior to the enactment of the Mosaic covenant, various reasons may have been given for avoiding this or that activity, including pragmatic justification for execution, in some cases. For example, blood revenge against a killer may have been thought necessary in order to maintain the balance of power between clans. Similarly, refusal to obey the judicial decisions of the highest court could not be tolerated if there was to be an orderly society.

Under the covenant initiated at Mount Sinai, however, such older motivations became secondary. It was sufficient to explain all penalties as the consequence of violation of the covenant relationship. Thus, here and there in the text (preceding or following a specific regulation), there will be a quick reminder of the overall picture: "I am the Lord your God," the very words with which the covenant formultion began at Exodus 20:2 (so Lev. 18:2, 30; 19:4, 10, 12; 23:43). It is interesting to note that this reminder (justification) is concentrated in the so-called priestly literature (see Appendix A), which contains many requirements which, to the modern mind, may seem unduly restrictive or lacking in compelling logical justification (e.g., bestiality, homosexuality). Thus, that which one might most easily wish to ignore is that which is most clearly subject to divine authority.

Therefore, crimes which undermined the existence of the community, which treated God's manifest graciousness with indifference, which turned the community's oath of loyalty (Josh. 24) into a lie, could be taken to justify the death penalty. It was not so much that a specific act was intrinsically wrong, or that it had negative practical consequences. Rather, certain acts were evidence of ingratitude, infidelity to one's oath, rebellion, and (in the last analysis) an attack upon God (if not atheism).

The priestly regulations, standing at the culmination of Pentateuchal development, uniquely stress a new motivation for obedience: holiness. Why does one follow a certain life-style and avoid others? Because the Deity invites one to live in imitation of the divine nature: "You shall be holy, for I the Lord your God am holy" (Lev. 19:2; 20:26, etc.). Basic to the idea of holiness is separation, distinction: "And you shall not walk in the customs of the nation which I am casting out before you; for they did all these [forbidden] things, and therefore I abhorred them. . . . I am the Lord your God, who have separated you from the peoples. . . . You shall be holy to me" (Lev. 20:23-26). Activities, therefore, which breach that wall of distinction destroy the People of God and are a renunciation of its Sovereign Lord.

In the case of murder the biblical materials (and the priestly regulations in particular) offer the clearest and most sustained justification of the death penalty, the very issue around which the modern debate has raged.

Israel's priestly theologians were much concerned to regulate human activities in which blood was involved. That there was a connection between life and blood was obvious: As blood flowed from the body, the organism grew progressively weaker until death resulted. It seemed obvious, therefore, that the life-force resided in the blood: "for the life of the flesh is in the blood" (Lev. 17:11). Not surprisingly, therefore, in some societies ancient (e.g., Greece) and modern (e.g., New Guinea), blood was deliberately consumed in order to incorporate the life-force of the victim (whether animal or human) into that of the consumer. While persons in Israel may not have sought to consume blood for that reason, it is clear that it was nonetheless considered to be an arrogant act. Life originated by a special act of the Deity (by the power of the divine breath, as the ancient story in Gen. 2:7 put it). Consequently, humans were not free to terminate it, save under conditions specified by God. Even food animals must be brought to the sanctuary and slaughtered in a prescribed ritual whereby the blood is removed. Failure to do so results in "bloodguilt" (Lev. 17:4), a term which is elsewhere used for the murder of a human being (Exod. 22:2). How much more the offense, therefore, if human life ("created in the image of God," Gen. 1:26) is taken without proper sanction! One has acted arrogantly against a life-force that is an extension of God's own life-giving power. It is, to put it baldly, "an attack upon God" (Patrick, p. 72). Even an animal who kills a human is to be destroyed (Exod. 21:28). A human who does so all the more forfeits any right to life (Gen. 9:1-7). No alternative is to be allowed (Num. 35:31) and the community must not be swayed by values to the contrary: "Your eye shall not pity. . ." Such modern rationalizations as, What good would it do to take the murderer's life? Does it bring the victim back? are beside the point. Nor would it be accurate to characterize the Bible's point of view here as the type of retaliation or vengeance that is unfitting of sensitive religious persons (and which Christianity supposedly would forbid). The murderer is no longer to be executed in order to satisfy the demands of family or clan. It is the Deity who makes the demand as the Lord of Life. Is compensation due for the loss which the Deity has suffered? (Phillips, pp. 95-99)

CHAPTER III

Some Traditional Demurs

When Scripture is invoked in a discussion of capital punishment, advocates usually appeal to the Hebrew Bible, while opponents concentrate upon the New Testament. We will turn to the question of the correctness of this supposed contrast in part 2. In the meanwhile, attention needs to be focused upon a few texts which might seem to be out of conformity with the overall approach of the Hebrew Bible.

1. There is the sixth of the Ten Commandments (the fifth commandment, as Roman Catholics and Lutherans number them), which seems to state, categorically, "You shall not kill" (Exod. 20:13; Deut. 5:17). Does that forbid execution? To this complex issue, deserving of detailed discussion we shall turn in chapter 4.

2. God said to Noah, "Whoever sheds the blood of man, by man shall his blood be shed" (Gen. 9:6). Is that possibly a predictive statement (or observation about reality), rather than a prescriptive (legislative) one? That is, just as Jesus observed that "all who take the sword will perish by the sword" (Matt. 26:52), without thereby sanctioning execution, so perhaps God is merely commenting upon the way that the world will work and not ordering any action on society's part. So argued Charles Spear amidst a mid–nineteenth-century

debate about capital punishment (*Essays on the Punishment of Death,* cited in Megivern, p. 147).

While Genesis 9:6, standing in isolation, might be taken in either of these senses, no such ambiguity remains when it is considered in context. The passage begins with imperatives (9:1 ff.) and continues with prohibitions (9:4), making it clear that the Deity is directing, not laconically describing reality. No doubt remains after the statement, "For your lifeblood I will surely require a reckoning" (v. 5). The King James Version is a bit more literal: "And surely your blood of your lives will I require," making it quite clear what the nature of the Revised Standard Version's "reckoning" is.

3. When the murderer Cain fears that "whoever finds me will slay me" (Gen. 4:14), the Deity places him under special protection, "lest any who came upon him should kill him" (v. 15). It could thus be argued that, in contrast to the requirements of Moses and to the practice of the later Israelites, here we have the ultimate model for response to the situation: The Deity evidences graciousness in response to the plea of the first murderer! Such a possible precedent for judicial behavior in the present was heard by George Cheever, writing only a short time before Spear (*Punishment by Death: Its Authority and Expediency,* cited in Megivern, p. 146). This point of view was recently advocated by a seminary professor of Christian ethics (Milligan, p. 176).

Cheever's reason for rejecting this interpretation is in keeping with his book's title. It runs as follows: Look what happened as a consequence of the failure to exterminate the line of Cain! It led to the corruption of the world at the time of Noah, and necessitated the flood. It was an inadequate reason for rejection (touching on God's incompetence), as his critics (including Spear) were quick to point out. Nonetheless, Cheever's rejection of the interpretation was entirely merited.

The purpose of the Cain and Abel story, from the point of view of modern scholarship within the church and synagogue, will seem quite alien to the average reader, and there is space here to sketch it only in broad outline. The story, standing alone, is apparently a folk-explanation for the traveling metallurgist of the ancient Near East, "wandering" (Gen. 4:16, RSV footnote) from village to village in order to ply his trade. Indeed, the word "cain" means something like "blacksmith" in Hebrew. Members of this guild wore a sign (tattoo?) on their foreheads to signify their protection by the gods of the underworld into whose realm they had descended in order to learn their skills and from which they secured rock with which to make metal. The story thus explains how, in primeval time, the first metallurgist ("Cain") received his sign of protection and why he "wanders" over the earth.

However, Israel's theologians have placed the story in a larger context, which stretches from creation to the call of Abraham, and thereby have given it a new meaning: The status of human beings after their relationship with God has been strained to the limit. In no case, therefore, does the story have to do with what society ought to do with murderers. (Those wishing to pursue this biblical chapter further should begin by coming to an understanding of the type of literature that this is: See the article by Priest. Then, one must learn something of the status of the metallurgist in the ancient Near East; see, e.g., Gaster, pp. 51-75. Finally, in order to understand the use to which the ancient story has been put in Israel's sacred literature as it now stands, see, e.g., von Rad, pp. 99-106.)

The understanding against which Cheever argues illustrates well a rule of interpretation which will serve us later when we study the story of Jesus and "the woman taken in adultery" (John 8:3-11; see chapter 9). And that rule is this: Beware of extracting rules for moral behavior from events in a narrative! For moral guidance, we should turn to materials that are instructional in form (e.g., the Ten Commandments, or the Sermon on the Mount).

4. Since most modern advocates of the death penalty for murder cite the Bible but do not insist upon this penalty for all the crimes for which Scripture mandates it, is there not a problem of inconsistency? Thus Dr. Benjamin Rush observed, as part of the first great debate on the topic in the newly formed United States: "If the Mosaic law with respect to murder be obligatory upon Christians, it follows that it is equally obligatory upon them to punish harlotry, blasphemy, and the other capital crimes that are mentioned in the Levitical law by death" (*Considerations on the Injustice and Impolicy of Punishing Murder by Death*, 1792, cited in Megivern, p. 144).

This is a refrain that is almost certain to surface in any contemporary discussion of the topic. It should be clear, however, upon a moment's reflection, that the "inconsistency" has no bearing upon the witness of the Bible. While it may present a problem for advocates of capital punishment and one which they need to clarify, it does not arise merely from the preferences or social conditioning of the advocate, since it has its roots in the biblical tradition. The Bible itself singles out murder for special condemnation, and permits no compensation or pity. Westermann (p. 468), a foremost interpreter of Genesis, is surely right when he says: "Here in Genesis 9 murder is something utterly on its own; nothing can be compared with it. Throughout the whole sweep of human history, the murderer by his action despoils God." Moreover, while Jesus apparently felt free to set aside certain traditional regulations pertaining to "clean" and "unclean" foods, he did not do so for the regulaton concerning murder. He is no more and no less guilty of "inconsistency" than are modern advocates of the death penalty. (See the discussion of John 8:3-11 in chapter 9.)

5. The prophet Ezekiel announces to the exiles, "As I live, says the Lord God, I have no pleasure in the death of the wicked, but that the wicked turn from his way and live; turn back, turn back from your evil ways; for why will you die, O

house of Israel?" (33:11) To some readers, that may seem clear enough! God not only takes no "pleasure" in the death (execution?) of the "wicked" (criminal?), but prefers that they "turn back" (be rehabilitated?).

Such an understanding might indeed be justified if one could read the Bible atomistically, that is, a verse at a time, with the understanding that the verse has a self-contained eternal truth. However, if the prophet is speaking to a specific audience about a particular problem, and if his response covers several verses (or even a chapter), then the modern interpreter must hear him out and look for the central idea. That is, what a verse *says* may not be what the context (and thus the prophet) *means*.

In contrast to the King James Version, which prints each verse as if it were a separate paragraph, other translations may group verses together into larger thought-units (paragraphs). Thus, the Revised Standard Version divides Ezekiel 33 into the following units: verses 1-6, 7-9, 10-16, 17-20, 21-22, 23-29, and 30-33. One of the reasons for such division is the Deity's address to the prophet, "Son of man" (vv. 2, 7, 10, 23, 30). Curiously, the Revised Standard Version ignores one such address as the indication of a new speech: verse 12. By contrast, the New English Bible puts a division there, indicating that verses 10-11 go together (so also NAB, TEV, NIV). It thus becomes clear that the words are addressed to "the house of Israel" (a wider reading reveals that these are the Judean exiles in Babylonia), in response to their lament that "our transgressions . . . are upon us, and we waste away . . . how can we live?" (Ezek. 33:10). The Deity's response, then, is directed to those exiles, who are despondent about the possibility of ever returning to their homeland. Word has reached them that the city of Jerusalem, the center of their hope for return, has fallen into the hands of the Babylonians (v. 21).

Who are the wicked? The exiles whose betrayal of the covenant has led to exile. What is meant by their "death"?

Both their political situation ("we waste away") and their dwindling faith in the ancient concept of election. Thus they ask, "How can we live?" (i.e., keep our faith and identity as the People of God). God takes no "pleasure" in the death of the wicked (i.e., does not see it as necessary that the exiles have this attitude and forever remain in Babylonia). The Deity desires repentance, change of priorities, renewal of ancient values, life as it was intended by this community, and (at the appropriate time) return to the "promised land."

Thus, the text is not concerned with the fate of anyone who has been sentenced to death by the judiciary (or even per se with individuals who face death), and it does not therefore suggest what the religious person's response should be in that case.

CHAPTER IV

The Sixth Commandment

*U*nderstandably, the traditional confusion about the attitude of the Hebrew Bible toward capital punishment arises from the sixth of the Ten Commandments. In the classic English version (KJV and others) we read, "Thou shalt not kill" (Exod. 20:13; Deut. 5:17). "Kill," as a comprehensive term, does not distinguish between accident (involuntary manslaughter), malice (murder), self-defense, legal execution, or death in battle. Since no object is specified (humans), it could be argued that this is an absolute prohibition against the ending of any life, animal or human (Nahmani). As such, the commandment would seem to be in tension with the death sentences which we have previously reviewed, as well as with the frequent commands for Israel to enter into battle with enemies (e.g., Exod. 17:8-13; Deut. 20:10-18). The situation seems especially puzzling in view of the fact that it is the same Moses who says, "You shall not kill" and (a mere chapter later), "Whoever strikes his father or his mother shall be put to death" (Exod. 21:15).

It is suprising that many readers do not discover this "problem" on their own; indeed, students in seminary are sometimes astonished when it is pointed out to them. Such blindness results from the tendency to read the Bible as if each sentence stands on its own, with a self-contained truth.

There supposedly is no need to study the larger context. Thus, if the text says, "You shall not kill," then that is the way it is! Should a tension be sensed with another text, then the fault must lie in our inadequate understanding: "Somehow, it is all OK!"

Readers of some recent versions of the Bible (new translations such as TEV, rather than revisions of earlier ones such as KJV and RSV) have been surprised to find that the commandment reads, "You shall not commit murder" (so NEB; see also NIV, NJV, TEV). That the issue is not settled, however, is suggested by the fact that other recent translations continue the traditional wording (JB, NAB).

The problem resides in the fact that the verb (Hebrew *r-ts-ch*) does not evidence a single narrow and precise meaning in its forty-six occurrences in the Bible. Hence even the King James Version rendered it, at one place or another, as "kill" (I Kings 21:19), "murder" (Jer. 7:9), "put to death" (Num. 35:30), and "slay" (Deut. 22:26). Complicating things even more is the fact that a number of other verbs are rendered "to kill" at one place or another by the King James Version, among them *h-r-g, z-b-ch, ch-l-l, t-b-ch, m-w-t, n-k-h, q-t-l,* and *sh-ch-t.* May one assume that the types of "killing" which all those verbs denote are different from what the commandment forbids by the verb *r-ts-ch?*

No wonder that the careful reader of the Bible may end up in a state of confusion, and that the same text (the sixth commandment) was used by both the prosecutor and the defense attorney in the trial which I witnessed as a child (see the Introduction).

Whatever the meaning of the commandment may be, it is helpful to realize that it does not use the customary vocabulary (verb) for execution or killing in battle. In the former case, the verb of choice is usually *m-w-t* ("to die"). Hence, in the series of capital offenses outlined in Exodus 21 and in Leviticus 20, the refrain is *môt yûmat,* "he shall be put to death." In the latter case, the customary verb is *n-k-h* ("to smite").

What, then, does the commandment mean? Sometimes the verb *r-ts-ch* is used to describe an unintentional killing (Deut. 4:41-42). It does not seem likely, however, that the commandment would seek to forbid accidents. In other cases, the verb is used for sanctioned execution (Num. 35:30, "shall be put to death"). If the commandment forbids that, then it is in tension with clear divine mandate elsewhere in Scripture. In yet other cases, the verb seems to describe premeditated murder (Ps. 94:4-7; Hos. 6:9). The verb seemingly is used in that sense by the prophets, who condemn such action in the strongest of terms (Jer. 7:9; Hos. 4:2).

In view of such diverse usage, the following solutions have been offered:

1. Given the range of usage and the imprecision in individual texts, it is impossible to know what the commandment intends. (It may be for this reason that some recent translations continue to use the term "kill": Not that they take the commandment to be an absolute prohibition of taking human life, but that they prefer latitude to precision in view of the linguistic uncertainty.)

2. Given the wide range of individual usages, it is preferable to incorporate them all into a comprehensive meaning: It *is* an absolute prohibition against the taking of human life. It is a pristine Mosaic ideal which was soon given up. Texts which allow killing in battle or which order the execution of criminals are thus a later and degenerate form of Israel's religion. They do not represent the values of the historical Moses. (Such an approach has only been offered by an occasional solitary voice.)

3. The verb *r-ts-ch,* rather than having all its attested meanings at the same period in Israel's history, has developed meanings with the passage of time (just as words do in any language). The early meaning was the taking of human life which necessitated execution by the "avenger of blood" (i.e., the question of the killer's motives was irrelevant). The later meaning injects the motive of malice

and violence (murder). It is the later meaning which the commandment has in mind (Childs, p. 421). (Since the date of the formation of the commandments is itself vigorously debated, such an argument is not without its problems, especially if one wishes to date them earlier, i.e., to the Mosaic period.)

4. The meaning of the commandment cannot be decided on linguistic grounds (vocabulary and grammar), but only by placing it within the context of other Pentateuchal legislation (especially from the same period from which the commandments are presumed to have originated). It is a context in which killing in battle and execution for capital offense is clearly and repeatedly mandated. The larger historical and literary context (Joshua–Kings and the prophetic books) reveals a strong aversion to the *malicious* taking of human life. Thus, there is clearly socially sanctioned killing, and there is forbidden killing. The term "murder," however imprecise it may be, is thus preferable to any other.

This last solution might cause the conscientious reader of the Bible to breathe a sign of relief: The tension between the commandment and the demands for execution elsewhere in Scripture has resulted from translators' lack of precision, and does not necessarily reside within the text itself.

The closest parallels to the commandment are the following:

"Whoever strikes a man so that he dies shall be put to death."

(Exod. 21:12)

"Cursed be he who slays his neighbor in secret."

(Deut. 27:24)

"He who kills a man shall be put to death."

(Lev. 24:17)

What is it that the person has done in these cases to merit death? Despite the differing translations ("strikes," "slays," "kills"), the Hebrew verb is the same in each case *(n-k-h)*. It is a verb which suggests attack, striking, violence, intention, malice. It is, therefore, the verb of choice for describing death in battle (II Sam. 2:23; 20:10) but is by no means limited to that situation (I Sam. 17:35) or even to a fatality (Exod. 2:11, 13; hence the added stipulation above in Exod. 21:12, "so that he dies"). Hence the King James Version prefers to render it by "to smite" (including at two of the texts quoted above). Note especially that Deuteronomy adds the phrase "in secret," suggesting that the life was not taken within the bounds of social sanction.

One may plausibly suggest, therefore, that the concern of the commandment *(r-ts-ch)* is closely related to, if not identical with, the concern of the other three texts *(n-k-h)*. That is, it forbids premeditated, malicious violence that is not sanctioned by divine decree as mediated by the stipulations of Israel's covenant.

Discontinuity with the Past?

Modern Christians who oppose capital punishment on scriptural grounds center their appeal on the text of the New Testament. This they do for one or more of the following reasons.

1. The church has traditionally distinguished the tone of the New Testament from that of the Hebrew Bible: The former is characterized by "gospel" whereas the latter has a tendency toward "law." One should expect, therefore, a greater emphasis upon God's graciousness in its pages and less upon the kind of "justice" which capital punishment presupposes.

Such a distinction is questionable, however. "Law" is not a designation which either Testament applies to the Hebrew Bible as a whole. Its use to translate the Hebrew word *torah* and the Greek word *nomos* is linguistically doubtful (Sanders) and creates a prejudice in the mind of the reader. It is evident, at a fair reading, that God's graciousness is as evident in the older part of Scripture as it is in the newer (Holladay). Indeed, the ancient creedal affirmation of God's nature, often cited in the Hebrew Bible, is, "The Lord, the Lord, a God merciful and gracious, slow to anger, and abounding in steadfast love and faithfulness, keeping steadfast love for thousands, forgiving iniquity and transgression and sin" (so the formative theophany at Mount Sinai, Exod. 34:6-7).

It is instructive to note not only the "limitations and safeguards" (outlined above in chapter 1) but also the humaneness which characterized the judicial system of the People of God (ancient Israel). Only a few examples need be cited here: (a) The punishment for an offense cannot exceed the crime. That is the intention of the famous *lex talionis* (law of reciprocal punishment): "an eye for an eye." This has been perverted, in common understanding, into an act of cruelty. Properly understood, it intends to limit the excesses which codes in the ancient Near East allowed. Thus one might translate, "[Only] fracture for fracture, eye for eye, tooth for tooth" (Lev. 24:20; see Renger). (b) Corporal punishment is strictly limited, lest its recipients be degraded (Deut. 25:1-3).

Anyone who is informed concerning the brutality which characterized the ancient world (from Babylonia to Rome) and parts of the modern scene (including colonial America) will applaud the evaluation found at Deuteronomy 4:8, "And what great nation is there, that has statues and ordinances so righteous as all this law *(torah)* which I set before you this day?" It has always seemed to me to be the perfect illustration of Matthew 7:3-5 ("first take the log out of your own eye") that the modern followers of Jesus view the New Testament's threats of eternal torture in hell as somehow admirably gracious in comparison with the Hebrew Bible. My point here is not one of criticism of the New Testament, but of the capricious, self-serving way in which some interpreters approach it.

2. Jesus' saying, "You have heard that it was said . . . But I say" (Matt. 5:21-22, 27-28, 31-32, 33-34, 38-39, 43-44) has been taken to indicate the obsolescence of the Pentateuchal guidelines.

However, this overlooks the fact that, in the introduction to this section (vv. 17-20), Jesus states that he has come not "to abolish the law *(nomos)* and the prophets . . . but to fulfill them." He then takes several traditional guidelines and gives them an even more demanding interpretation than was spelled out in the original! Rather than releasing one from prior obligation, he is a "hard liner" who makes things even tougher.

However, the situation is clouded a bit by occasions when Jesus renounced other Pentateuchal restrictions. According to Mark 7:19, "He declared all foods clean" (see also Matt. 15:11-18). This would seem to be a rejection of the regulations in Leviticus 11. Conversely, he advised that other Levitical guidelines be obeyed (so Matt. 8:1-4; Luke 17:11-14, concerning skin irregularities).

What, then, was his attitude toward Pentateuchal regulation of murder—the stringent approach of Matthew 5, or the rebellious approach of Matthew 15 and Mark 7? Curiously, the only quotation which touches on the matter comes from Matthew 15 (vv. 1-9). His opponents have accused his disciples of violating a religious regulation. He replies that it is merely a "tradition of the elders" which is being waived, whereas his opponents are ignoring something far more serious: "For *God* commanded, 'Honor your father and your mother,' and 'He who speaks evil of father or mother, let him surely die.' But you say, 'If . . . , he need not honor his father.' So, for the sake of your tradition, you have made void the word of God." He thus refers to the regulation in Exodus 21:17 and Leviticus 20, concerning honor due one's parents. Does he thereby attest to a belief in the continuing validity of the death penalty, at least for the offense stated? (There is a question of interpretation here: The central issue is the hypocrisy of his opponents. See the discussion of John 8:3-11 in chapter 9.)

3. The entirety of the Mosaic legislation was historically conditioned and meant for temporary duration: In the absence of anything better, it would do until the coming of the Messiah, when a superior (and ultimate) ethical system would be offered. Thus, it served as a propaedeutic (preparatory instruction) for the gospel.

This rather self-serving argument may have had its basis in a limited argument by Jesus concerning divorce (Matt. 19:3-9). He was asked if divorcing one's wife was lawful, the rumor apparently being that he had spoken against divorce (whereas Deut. 24:1-4 sanctioned it). He explained the Mosaic permissiveness in this way: "For your hardness of heart Moses allowed you to divorce your wives," that is, it was a temporary concession to the reality of human (male?) weakness.

What Jesus did on a limited scale, the early church applied with gusto: The entire *torah* had served its purpose and was no longer of ultimate authority. Unfortunately, such scope overlooks the grounds upon which Jesus had reached his decision concerning divorce: "From the beginning, it was not so." He thus appeals to Genesis 1–2, where God "from the beginning made them male and female" and "the two shall become one," and concludes, "What therefore God has joined together, let no man put asunder."

Jesus' appeal to an earlier *torah* episode, presumably aimed at humanity rather than at Israel (as was the case with the Mosaic materials), was precisely the approach taken by the rabbis in replying to the propaedeutic argument: *torah* was already known to the patriarchs, and Moses merely codified it (so *Sifre* Deut.; see John 7:22, where RSV's "fathers" refers to the patriarchs).

If one tries to set aside the regulations concerning capital punishment which are concentrated in the Mosaic *torah* and aimed specifically at Israel, one runs headlong into the reality of Genesis 9, given (as the text now stands) much earlier and aimed at the entire human race.

A radical variation upon the ancient propaedeutic argument has been advanced in recent days: The biblical approval of execution reflects the justifiable penology of its times. Perhaps the following expression is characteristic of this point of view:

> When the legal precedents of the Torah were formulated, capital punishment was an absolute necessity. The denial of such a punishment would doubtless have meant not better justice, but a return to older tribal patterns of revenge. The question we must ask is, do the reasons for the use of capital punishment during the biblical period still exist? And further, does this form of punishment accomplish what it sets out to do? Does it really act as a deterrent for future crimes? Is it the only recourse by which a society can be preserved and individuals protected? . . .
>
> These are questions which must be answered, in part, by the sociologists. (Williams, pp. 182-83)

Unfortunately, this approach reflects a number of serious misunderstandings, among them the following: (a) Capital punishment, in Israel, was not instituted as a means of controlling "older tribal patterns of revenge." Rather, such tribal activity was itself socially sanctioned execution. True, the cities of refuge (Num. 35) later seek to regulate it, but this makes it all the clearer that execution in the case of murder (as opposed to homicide) has social sanction. (b) In relation to reasons and accomplishments, only the issue of deterrence is mentioned here. However, this is nowhere close to the center of the Bible's concern, as we have seen (chapter 2). Rather, the issue with respect to murder is God's fundamental claim as the Lord of Life. What the sentence seeks to accomplish, therefore, is to obey God who has been wronged by such an attack. Does that reason still exist? To my knowledge, God has never given a canonical indication to the contrary.

From the Bible's point of view, therefore, it is utterly astonishing for an appeal to be made to sociological research for insight on the matter (namely, does the specified punishment deter?) However, as we will see later, this is precisely the kind of appeal which some modern Christian groups have made (chapter 12). Thereby theology is reduced to a matter of utilitarian self-interest.

4. There are several passages which have been taken to bear directly or indirectly upon Jesus' attitude toward capital

punishment (and thereby to indicate the attitude which his followers should have in the present). Herein lies the heart of the matter. For example, there seemingly are warnings against being judgmental (Matt. 7:1), and exhortations are given that one should be forgiving and loving (Matt. 5:38-48). In addition, there is an episode in which Jesus was asked directly about what was to be done with a person who had been apprehended in a capital offense (John 8:3-11). Discussion of texts of this type may be found below, in chapter 9.

CHAPTER VI

Jurisdiction

*A*n accurate portrait of jurisdiction for capital crimes during the New Testament period has long been obscured by a number of factors. Foremost among them is the fact that the background materials are written in rabbinic Hebrew and Talmudic Aramaic and are located in a voluminous literature which Christian interpreters were usually ill-equipped to handle. Thus, clarification for English-reading Christians has come only in the last few decades. Compounding the difficulty is the fact that the Evangelists do not clearly distinguish political and religious charges, that is, the concerns of Rome from those of the Synagogue. Confusion is added by the inconsistency with which translations of the Bible render the designations of the various jurisdictions. For example, Jesus (and several of his followers) are examined by a group called (in Greek) a *sunedrion* (which has come into English as sanhedrin). The King James Version renders the term, in all twenty-two of its occurrences, as "council." Clear enough! However, it also renders *sumboulion* in the same way. Are the two really the same institution? Then, there is a *gerousia* before which investigation took place, rendered as "senate." The Revised Standard Version renders both *sunedrion* and *sumboulion* as "council," and then adds to them *bouletes* (a member of the *boule*), "member of the council" (KJV: "counselor").

When clarification of jurisdiction began to be presented in English (Zeitlin), it was handicapped by the proposal that there were two sanhedrins: a religious one and a political one. The former was furthermore of two types: a Great Sanhedrin of seventy-one judges and several Small Sanhedrins of twenty-three judges. The "religious" body was known (in Hebrew) as a *bet-din* ("court") prior to 70 C.E. but was also known as a sanhedrin thereafter. Little wonder, then, that there was confusion in the mind of the non-specialist reader about who crucified whom and for what.

The development of these jurisdictions was roughly as follows. When the Judean exiles returned from Babylonia (following the edict of Cyrus of Persia in 539 B.C.E.; II Chron. 36:22-23; Ezra 1:1-4), monarchy was abolished and Judah became a theocracy as part of the Persian Empire. That is, leadership was in the hands of the Aaronide High Priest, guided by the Pentateuch save in matters pertaining to the interests of Persia. When he needed advice in religious matters, he might convene a group of scholars which tradition has come to call "the Great Synagogue." In matters of civil (Persian) interest, he might assemble representatives of the aristocracy to meet in council *(gerousia)*.

The Maccabean Revolt (168–165 B.C.E.) ended foreign domination (by now, from the Greeks), and it also brought the wide-ranging power of the High Priest to an end. The High Priest retained control over the functioning of the temple, but not over religious policy-making or over the administration of justice. Those duties were given to two levels of courts *(bet-din)*: a "great" one for policy-making, and "small" ones for administration (trials). By contrast, violators of the laws of the state (headed initially by the Maccabees/ Hasmoneans, then by the Herodians) were tried by a council called a *sunedrion* (literally: "seated together," perhaps borrowed from Hellenized Egyptian governance).

The "great" *bet-din*, meeting regularly in Jerusalem, gave interpretations based upon *torah* that were binding upon Jews throughout the world and which served to guide the judges of a "small" *bet-din* (one of which existed in every city of size). It was in the latter courts that capital cases would have been tried (e.g., murder). Both courts were thus independent of civil authority and conversely had no jurisdiction over political prisoners.

A *sunedrion*, by contrast, was an ad hoc body, called into session as needed by the ruler to deal with activities that undermined the welfare of the state.

Membership of the *bet-din* was Pharisaic (i.e., experts in the interpretation of *torah*), headed by a *nasi* (president) and an *ab bet-din* (vice-president). Membership of a *sunedrion* was made up of the "leading citizens": those whose social, financial, and political interests were compatible with the status quo. This would include the High Priest (a political appointment in the late pre-Maccabean period and under the Roman procurators), members of the priestly (Sadducean) family, representatives of the bureaucracy of monarchy (Herodians), and perhaps a few Pharisees. This body was not guided by strict procedure or by statute, but by what it perceived to be necessary for the common good. Its decisions were often arbitrary, depending upon the whim of the ruler.

When the Romans took direct control of Judea (with the introduction of the system of procurators in 6 c.e.), the *sunedrion* became an instrument of the Caesar's justice. The procurators designated the High Priest to preside and to contain problems (e.g., revolutionaries) so that Roman power would not need to be used directly. Thus, in this period the sanhedrin was not an autonomous Jewish institution and it in no wise represented the sentiments of the masses.

With the destruction of the Temple (and thus the cessation of the office of High Priest), as a result of the failure of the (first) Jewish revolt (70 c.e.), the Romans then vested both political oversight and continuing religious power in the

Pharisaic *bet-din,* which now could be (and was) designated a *sunedrion.* Thus began the identification of the religious court with the term "sanhedrin," and then the projection of that identification backward into the period before 70 C.E., leading to the mistaken idea that it was a religious court which tried Jesus and many of his followers. It is an error that has contributed much to the long and tragic abuse of Jews at the hands of the church. (For further reading on this topic, see Appendix C.)

CHAPTER VII

The Practice

*T*he casual reader of the Bible will also be aware that capital punishment was carried out "in the land of the Bible" (Judah/Judea) during the time of the New Testament. The most conspicuous case, of course, was the execution of Jesus. There are, in addition, a number of lesser known instances. Among them are the following: two robbers crucified with Jesus (Matt. 27:38); Stephen (Acts 6:8-14; 7:58; whether this is a judicial act or mob action has been debated); and an unknown number of persons (Acts 26:9-11). Mention may also be made of trials on capital charges which did not result in conviction (Acts 5:17-40; 21:27–26:32), execution by decree of the secular ruler (Matt. 14:1-12), and instances outside Judea (Acts 14:19). Abundant additional examples may be found in the writings of the contemporary historian Josephus and in the rabbinic literature. (Briefly, see Greenberg's article "Crimes and Punishments," section E.)

Capital Offenses

The New Testament, unlike the Hebrew Bible, does not contain sections of legislation. Rather, amidst its narratives it contains exhortations to the followers of Jesus to live saintly lives as part of the Jewish community under Roman domination. Capital crimes, then, would be defined by (1) the Hebrew Bible, as now refined and interpreted through the lens of the oral *torah* (Mishnah) by the rabbinic courts, and (2) the Roman overlords, ruling through the Herodian monarchs, or a local council headed by the High Priest, or the procurators (e.g., Pontius Pilate).

From the former source arose charges of trespass upon sacred area (Acts 21:27-31), adultery (John 8:3-11), and blasphemy (Acts 6:11–7:58; 26:9-11). The last of these charges seems to have been leveled against Jesus also (Matt. 9:3; 26:65; John 10:33). The definition of the crime seems far looser than either the original statute or contemporary rabbinic interpretation (see Mishnah *Sanhedrin* 7.5), which required that the Holy Name must actually be pronounced by the accused, which apparently neither Jesus nor Stephen did. This was not, however, the charge which led to Jesus' execution (see Appendix C).

From the Roman government and its representatives will have arisen the charges of violation of public order (e.g., brigandage; Matt. 27:38), and sedition (by John the Baptist; Matt. 14:10, supported by the account of Josephus). Its courts also sentenced to death Jesus, Peter, and Paul (the last two suggested by post-biblical sources).

Methods of Execution

For religious crimes (i.e., under Jewish regulation), stoning remained the standard means, although others mentioned in the Hebrew Bible are attested (e.g., burning). Rabbinic literature (specifically in Mishnah *Sanhedrin*) also specifies strangulation and beheading (7.1). It was by the latter means that the murderer was to be dispatched (9.1), probably because of the precedent set in the Hebrew Bible where the murderer is to be hunted and struck down by the "avenger of blood" (Num. 35; see also chapter 1). For a few crimes in connection with the cult the offender might be clubbed to death on the spot (Mishnah *Sanhedrin* 9.6).

On the specific methods, it is conspicuous that only beheading will ensure the spilling of blood, a punishment otherwise reserved (in the Hebrew Bible) for the citizens of an apostate city. Israel's aversion to this method relates to the connection between blood and the life-force, a force which was identified with the power of God. It was thus a horrible fate, sanctioned by Genesis 9:6: "Whoever sheds the blood of man, by man shall his blood be shed."

For political crimes, death usually came by the sword (Matt. 14:10, in the case of John the Baptist) in the form of beheading (Rev. 20:4), or by crucifixion (in the case of Jesus).

CHAPTER VIII

The Rationale

*I*t is important to notice that the death penalty in Judea during the period of the New Testament was carried out by two judiciaries: (1) the Jewish religious courts *(bet-din)* for specified violations of *torah,* and (2) the Roman government, through its local appointees in council *(sunedrion),* for actions inimical to the peace.

Within the pages of the New Testament, there is no challenge to the legitimacy of the death penalty, per se, if exercised by either judiciary. While its writers may have believed that a given sentence was unjust (e.g., in the case of Jesus), that is quite different from rejecting execution within itself on theological (or any other) grounds.

For execution by sentence of the *bet-din,* no rationale need be stated. The understandings of ancient Israel (in the Hebrew Bible) would have carried over by canonical authority (i.e., as the Word of God through Moses, accepted by the community now for centuries). It is not surprising that Jesus the Jew would share that consensus. Thus, he stresses that no part of *torah* should be relaxed (Matt. 5:17-19), outlines applications that are deeper than are explicit in *torah* (5:21-48), appeals to the "law [*torah*] and the prophets" (7:12), instructs a leper concerning the observance of Levitical guidelines (8:1-4), instructs his followers to obey the teachings of Moses even as interpreted by the Pharisaic *bet-din* (23:1-3), cites *torah* in a discussion with the Sadducees (Mark 12:18-27), and instructs that the commandments must be kept if one "would enter life" (Matt. 19:16-17). One such reference specifically involves the death penalty (Matt. 15:4) for one who "curses his father or mother" (NEB).

For execution by the state (the Romans, through the *sunedrion*), one may also assume the continuation of older understandings and rationales. Within the period of the Hebrew Bible, Israel's monarchs formulated guidelines for the operation of the state, and this included execution of certain offenders. Indeed, Mosaic *torah* forbade cursing "a ruler of your people" (Exod. 22:28), and in this Paul concurred (Acts 23:1-5). It also legitimized the office of king, instructing the ruler to keep "all the words of this law [*torah*]" and to do them (Deut. 17:14-20). The prophetic corpus of Scripture, canonized later than the Pentateuch (i.e., in the second century B.C.E.), clearly undergirded the Judean monarchy with divine sanction, beginning with David (II Sam. 7). This then served to legitimate the return to monarchy at the time of the Hasmoneans and Herodians. Such kings then executed a number of persons, with never a protest that it was intrinsically improper for them to have done so. This does not mean, on the other hand, that every execution by monarchical decision was accepted as justified by the traditional religious leadership or was thought to be in accordance with Pentateuchal definitions. Indeed, there were vigorous protests in specific cases (e.g., II Sam. 11–12, where the prophet Nathan accuses David concerning Uriah the Hittite; I Kings 21, where Elijah announces God's death sentence upon King Ahab concerning the execution of Naboth). The existence of kingship in Israel is not only acknowledged as the will of God by the Wisdom Literature (Prov. 8:15-16), but it is lauded for the value which it may bring to society (Prov. 29:4). Indeed, one bold evaluation is:

"Inspired decisions are on the lips of a king; his mouth does not sin in judgment" (Prov. 16:10). The pragmatic value of civil government, even in the case of Rome, is likewise recognized by the author of I Peter: "Be subject for the Lord's sake to every human institution, whether it be to the emperor as supreme, or to governors as set by him to punish those who do wrong. . . . Fear God. Honor the emperor" (2:13-17).

Such theological appraisals and approvals of "law and order" do not indicate, within themselves, that the author is announcing, in the name of God, that capital punishment is thereby sanctioned. Nonetheless, while that is not explicitly stated here, it may well be implied, and indeed is in keeping with the totality of biblical thought.

All questions about the positive potential inherent in monarchy aside, there remained a basic theological question about foreign rule. Deuteronomy had specified that the king must be someone "whom the Lord your God will choose; one from among your brethren you shall set as king over you" (17:15). Presumably, this would ensure an awareness of the righteousness that was to characterize kingship. What, then, of the Romans, concerning whom the negative aspects were also becoming evident? To this various responses were possible. The first was to reject Roman rule on theological grounds, to the point of violence if necessary. This was the route chosen by the Sicarii (from their use of a short dagger, the *sica;* they are the historian Josephus' "fourth philosophy": *Antiquities,* 18.1.6; Acts 21:38, "assassins"). This led to the war of 70 c.e. and ultimately to the destruction of the Temple. The second response was anticipation of an inpending divine intervention which would sweep the Romans away, if not into hell. Such a radical apocalyptic point of view is reflected in the book of Revelation, whose author raves against the Empire, calling it (in the name of God) "mother of harlots and of earth's abominations. . . . drunk with the blood of saints" (17:1-6) and which is soon to be destroyed (18:1-24). A third response was to reach an uneasy accommodation with the

Romans, under the belief that they could not exercise sovereignty apart from the divine will that they do so. (For details, see chapter 9, the discussion of Matt. 5:43-48.) This approach, championed by the Pharisees, was articulated by Paul, a Roman citizen (Acts 22:27-28) who trusted in the Roman courts (Acts 25:8-12) and who had been brought up in the Pharisaic tradition (Acts 22:1-3; 23:6; Phil. 3:4-5). It is hardly surprising then that he would advise "all God's beloved in Rome": "Let every person be subject to the governing authorities. For there is no authority except from God, and those that exist have been instituted by God. Therefore he who resists the authorities resists what God has appointed, and those who resist will incur judgment. For rulers are not a terror to good conduct, but to bad. . . . He is the servant of God to execute his wrath on the wrongdoer" (Romans 13:1-4).

Such a perspective has antecedents in Israel's sacred literature. Jeremiah had advised the despondent exiles in Babylonia, "But seek the welfare of the city where I have sent you into exile, and pray to the Lord on its behalf, for in its welfare you will find your welfare" (29:7). Proverbs advanced the divine opinion that "by me kings reign, and rulers decree what is just" (8:15). The Wisdom of Solomon reminded kings and rulers over multitudes that "your dominion was given you from the Lord" (6:3).

CHAPTER IX

Some Misused Texts,
Pro and Con

A discussion of the New Testament perspective on capital punishment is likely to feature a small number of standard texts, interpreted in ways that are highly questionable. In some cases, the arguments are advanced by laypersons who have no formal training in the interpretation of Scripture, but in other cases by theologians who teach in institutions of higher learning.

Matthew 7:1

Jesus is sometimes quoted as having said, "Judge not!" The implication would be that this is an absolute prohibition.

Well, not quite! I have mentioned previously that there is a common tendency to read the sixth commandment in isolation from the larger context of the Pentateuch. In the present case, the tendency is carried even farther, when only part of a verse is considered authoritative. The full verse reads, "Judge not, that you be not judged." Even so, one still gets the impression from modern conversation that the entire verse was meant to be a condemnation of reaching a negative evaluation of anyone for anything: "If you don't want to be judged, then don't judge," or perhaps even, "God doesn't recommend that people make judgments." Hence even the dean of a theological seminary (Methodist) has stated, on the basis of this text, that the Christian "is warned that it is not for him to . . . judge the moral deserts of other persons."

The wider context makes the true meaning clear: "For with the judgment that you pronounce you will be judged, and the measure you give will be the measure you get" (v. 2). That is, one should not expect to be judged by God by a different standard than one customarily uses to judge others. Clear enough, and fair enough! This has no bearing, however, upon the undeniable *necessity* to judge others. Indeed, such judgment is something which the Bible repeatedly commands and which Moses, Jesus, and Paul regularly do. Nonetheless, the Bible stresses that judicial decrees within Israel must be fair and equitable. For example, "You shall appoint judges . . . and they shall judge the people with righteous judgment" (Deut. 16:18).

Does "righteous judgment" include the execution of a murderer? The Bible asserts this from beginning to end, without a single demur. The sentence is set by God's *torah,* and a judge cannot have discretion in the matter.

Jesus' words, in the text under discussion, concern interpersonal relationships between his disciples. They do not have the judicial system of the larger society in mind and thus should not be brought into a discussion of capital punishment.

Romans 1:26-32

Paul, having just listed a series of "unnatural" and "wicked" practices which characterize the pagan world, remarks, "Though they know God's decree that those who do such things deserve to die, they not only do them but approve those who practice them." This has been taken to mean that Paul sanctioned the execution of such persons.

The larger context is more complicated in this case, but it is no less helpful for correcting this erroneous interpretation.

Paul's preface to a discussion of God's offer of salvation begins with an analysis of the human situation (1:18–3:20). Following an indictment of pagan Hellenism (1:18-32), he suggests that the "unnatural" and "wicked" practices which he lists are symptoms of Hellenists' refusal to acknowledge the true God. Such persons could justifiably be left in the realm of death ("deserve to die") rather than be invited into the kingdom of God. The situation is not hopeless, however, because God has acted "in Jesus Christ" (3:21 ff.).

The understanding of death is this text is consistent with the apostle's use of the term throughout his writings (Bailey, *Biblical Perspectives*, pp. 87-91). Thus, the term should not be understood in the sense of execution such that the text supports capital punishment.

John 8:3-11

Jesus' attitude toward the "woman taken in adultery" (as the episode from John 8:3 KJV is commonly known) is likely the most frequently cited biblical evidence in the capital punishment debate. Perhaps the full text (8:3-11) is worth quoting.

> The scribes and the Pharisees brought a woman who had been caught in adultery, and placing her in the midst they said to him, "Teacher, this woman has been caught in the act of adultery. Now in the law Moses commanded us to stone such. What do you say about her?" This they said to test him, that they might have some charge to bring against him. Jesus bent down and wrote with his finger on the ground. And as they continued to ask him, he stood up and said to them, "Let him who is without sin among you be the first to throw a stone at her." . . . But when they heard it, they went away, one by one, beginning with the eldest, and Jesus was left alone with the woman standing before him. Jesus looked up and said to her, "Woman, where are they? Has no one condemned you?" She said, "No one, Lord." And Jesus said, "Neither do I condemn you; go, and do not sin again."

Jesus, so the reasoning goes, here manifests his mission to save the lost, to offer God's forgiveness rather than condemnation. His followers should use this text as a model for their own attitudes in the present, including setting aside demands for the death penalty. "Be like Jesus" would be the operative rule of interpretation.

Such an approach, however attractive it may be, should take into consideration at least the following cautions and obstacles.

1. There is a question of the authorship and date of the story. "This passage is not found in any of the important early Greek textual witnesses of Eastern provenance (e.g., in neither Bodmer papyrus); nor is it found in OS [Old Syriac] or the Coptic. . . . It is only from ca. 900 that it begins to appear in the standard Greek text." Clearly, "it was a later insertion" (Brown, p. 335). It is for this reason that some translations (e.g., the first edition of the RSV) place it as a footnote rather than as part of the text-proper. As an insertion, it may have been attracted to this particular location by verse 15, "You judge according to the flesh, I judge no one." However, a few ancient witnesses place it after 7:36 or at the end of the Gospel (as does NEB), and some of them after Luke 21:38 (perhaps because of similar entrapment stories in chapter 20). On the other hand, the story does occur in some Old Latin manuscripts, was known to Augustine, and was included in Jerome's Vulgate. Nonetheless, "In general the style is not Johannine either in vocabulary or grammar" (Brown, p. 336).

2. There is a question of the authority (canonization) of the story. If indeed it is a non-Johannine addition to the text, after the canon was agreed upon, does it have the status of Scripture? However, since it was included in the fourth-century Latin Vulgate, the Roman Catholic attitude has been one of acceptance. Since it later found its way into the Greek text as "received" by the Byzantine church and thence was translated by the English versions, it has found wide acceptance among Protestants as well.

3. There is a question of historicity. Even if this tradition is a stray narrative from genuine Johannine circles, that within itself may signal the need for caution. John's portrait of Jesus is much at variance with that of the other Gospels, as has been commonly observed. (For the difficulties involved, see Brown, pp. 336-37.)

4. There is a difficulty caused by the literary form of the account, narrative prose (story). What is its point? By contrast, one might note texts whose overt purpose is moral instruction. There is, for example, the Sermon on the Mount (Matt. 5–7), the purpose of which is to instruct hearers and which addresses them in the second person. The question of purpose is usually more difficult with narrative accounts and the present one is a good example. Was its purpose to indicate that the death penalty should be set aside as a matter of principle? Or was it to illustrate Jesus' mission to save the lost? Or was it to demonstrate his cleverness with respect to other religious leaders? Or was it to expose the motives of the woman's accusers? Has its purpose any relationship to a theme that seems to run from 5:1 to 10:42 (namely, controversy with opponents, whom he manages to best)?

That there are differing opinions about what this account "means" thus illustrates the value of a basic rabbinic rule for the interpretation of Scripture: One should not deduce *halakah* (ethical guidelines) from *haggadah* (scriptural narrative). Rather, ethical guidelines are to be sought in formal teachings, whose purpose is instruction in ethical behavior. One trusts in that which is clear and intentional, rather than that which is obscure and debatable.

5. There is the question of whether one ought to interpret and apply Scripture in accordance with its own intentions. (Whether one means thereby the intent of Jesus, or of the Johannine community which might have formulated and preserved the account, or of whoever might have inserted the story at precisely this location for editorial purposes, is beside the point here.) The alternative would be an *unintended*

meaning which the modern interpreter perceives and proposes: "I know this isn't what the text meant, but still, it's an edifying point of view, in keeping with where the Holy Spirit is leading now." My point of view is that interpreters ought to listen to the Bible's own agenda, rather than to squeeze from it implications for their own agenda!

The thrust of the story concerns the motives from which the accusers have brought the woman to Jesus. Had it merely been obedience to the historical norms of the community, they would have proceeded with her sentence. Rather, they have used her, with the collusion of her husband, for the purpose of entrapping a religious leader, an entrapment that could have very serious consequences. It is a shameful situation, far removed from the *torah*'s call for justice and righteousness, as the accusers quickly realized. Many rabbis at the time, had they been present and grasped the reality of the situation, would have joined Jesus in his assessment. There is, therefore, nothing uniquely "Christian" about his response. Rather, Jesus has listened to the Bible (the "Old Testament") with an intensity that his followers in the present would do well to begin to imitate.

It may be instructive to note, in view of the overall agenda of the account, that the particular prescribed punishment is entirely beside the point. Jesus' response would still be instructive (nothing crucial would have changed) if the charge had been that the husband had lain with his wife during her menstrual period (regulated by Lev. 15:19-24; 20:18), for which only corporal punishment was prescribed (Mishnah *Makkot*, 3.1). Should one argue, in that case, that Jesus implies that corporal punishment is wrong? Suppose that the crime were one for which only a fine was mandated? Should one then argue, on the basis of Jesus' response, that compensation is un-Christian?

6. May one indulge in substitution, as far as the woman's crime is concerned? May modern interpreters, in seeking a precedent for opposing capital punishment in the present,

substitute murder (the modern issue) for adultery? Would Jesus' response have been the same? To be precise about it, we cannot know for sure. Doubtless his observation of the accusers' motives would have been the same, with an attendant dissatisfaction on his part. Nonetheless, not all capital offenses were regarded as equally grave. Murder is singled out in the Bible as a crime for which monetary compensation was strictly forbidden (Num. 35:31), in apparent contrast to adultery (Prov. 6:32-35, where it is stated that the husband is unlikely to accept it). Insofar as the prophet Hosea's plea may be taken to reflect personal experience (as opposed to a depiction of the relationship between God and Israel), then whether or not to put his adulterous spouse to death was his decision to make rather than a mandatory one by society (Hos. 2:1-5; see also Num. 5:11-31 for such discretion, in contrast to Deut. 22:22). Murder is one of the few offenses concerning which Israel was enjoined, "Your eye shall not pity, but you shall purge the guilt of innocent blood from Israel" (Deut. 19:13). Whereas murder was understood to be an attack upon God (Gen. 9:5-6), adultery was initially understood only as an attack upon the husband's property (i.e., it must always involve a *married* female). One may wonder, therefore, if Jesus would have said to a murderer, "I do not condemn you!" (So also Ryrie, p. 214.) Thus, those who seek to use this text in the debate about execution of murderers have indulged in a bit of verbal sleight-of-hand, possibly in all innocence. (Nonetheless, during the Hadrianic persecutions of the second century C.E., the rabbis seem to have linked adultery with incest as one of the three cardinal sins which could not be excused even to save a human life, along with murder and idolatry. (See Babylonian Talmud, *Sanhedrin,* 74a; Jerusalem Talmud, *Sanhedrin,* 21b; *Sifra* on Lev. 16:16. Even so, in some cases a prior warning was necessary for conviction: Babylonian Talmud, *Sanhedrin,* 41a.)

7. May one take Jesus' response as a norm for all judicial

behavior? What would be the consequences if, in every case, the jurors were told, "Let him [or her] who is without sin . . . "? Presumably, Paul was right when he observed that "all have sinned" (Rom. 3:23; compare 5:12). Since we do not stone criminals any more, would we then be forced to remark, "Let the person without sin send this person to prison . . . demand compensation . . . or require rehabilitation and service in the community"? The result would be that no one could condemn anyone for anything! Thus the argument, when pursued to its logical conclusion, leads to an absurdity.

In conclusion, whatever Jesus' attitude toward capital punishment was, it cannot be detected from this passage. The oft-repeated claim that it can rests upon many questionable assumptions, one heaped upon the other: The text is a genuine report of Jesus' attitude; ethical directives can be derived from narrative, unambiguously; either the ethical directive of this story concerns the appropriateness of capital punishment, or one may ignore its point and propose one's own; what Jesus once did, he would do in every instance of the offense; Jesus' attitude in case of one offense would be the same for all offenses.

Surely Brown, a foremost interpreter of John, is right when he concludes, without stating his reasoning, "One should beware of attempts to make it [v. 7] a generalized norm forbidding enactments of capital punishment" (p. 338).

Matthew 5:43-48

If "the woman taken in adultery" is the most commonly cited biblical episode thought to bear on capital punishment, then surely Jesus' words at Matthew 5:43-48 are the most commonly quoted teaching: "Love your enemies and pray for those who persecute you, so that you may be sons of your Father who is in heaven. . . . You, therefore, must be perfect, as your heavenly Father is perfect." Since this advice is contrasted with an earlier (prevailing?) attitude ("You have heard that it was said, 'You shall love your neighbor and hate your enemy' "), and that attitude presumably included execution, might not Jesus' attitude demand clemency toward those accused of capital crimes?

It should be realized, first of all, that Jesus' contrast is not with the Hebrew Bible (which does not advise hating one's enemies), but with this ordinary tendency of human behavior: to disdain one's enemies and to favor one's friends. Rather, those who would be "sons" of God must pattern their behavior after that of the Deity "who makes his sun rise on the evil and on the good, and sends rain on the just and on the unjust" (v. 45). The call, therefore, is for mature action in the day-to-day events of ordinary life: to be without prejudice and devoid of self-interested motives. Thus, this is in keeping with the context of verses 17-42, where there are applications of *torah* that go beyond normal expectations: not merely slaying with weapons, but with words (vv. 21-26); not merely overt sexual activity, but inner intention (vv. 27-30).

To assume, in this context, that Jesus suddenly starts rejecting the moral regulations of *torah* concerning murder is little short of astonishing, especially in view of how the section begins ("Think not that I have come to abolish the law. . . . Whoever then relaxes one of the least of these commandments . . ."—vv. 17-18).

The intended application of Jesus' ethical teaching concerning love of enemies must be studied within the political context of his times. He instructs his followers (and all who would be "sons" of God) as an aberrant rabbi within a larger society that is under foreign (Roman) domination. He has no authority to judge criminal cases under either Jewish (the "small" *bet-din*) or Roman (the *sunedrion*) regulations. He has no *designated* authority even to interpret *torah* in relation to trials (i.e., he is not a member of the "great" *bet-din*). It is not surprising, therefore, that he has nothing *directly* to say about these matters.

The Pharisaic leaders, it would seem, came to an uneasy

accommodation with their Roman masters. Taxes would be paid, troops could be stationed, the peace would be maintained for them by the *sunedrion,* if nothing essential to Jewish life and worship would be encroached upon by the Romans. (To be sure, this accommodation had not come about without a certain number of confrontations, documented by the contemporaries Philo and Josephus. Nor did all Jewish groups accept it, foremost among them the Sicarii who precipitated the fatal revolt in 70 c.e.)

Echoes of the accommodation, and of the tension, may be heard in the episode about taxation (Matt. 22:15-22). When asked, "Is it lawful to pay taxes to Caesar, or not?" Jesus pointed to the surface of a Roman coin and replied, "Whose likeness and inscription is this?" When the questioners identified it as the Caesar's, he said, "Render therefore to Caesar the things that are Caesar's, and to God the things that are God's." In this regard he sounds like the quietistic faction of the Pharisees who turned from involvement in political affairs to the study and actualization of *torah* in their personal lives. For them, "governmental" problems were those of interpretation and application of *torah,* for which the *bet-din* ("great" and "small") was the instrument. The nitty-gritty of "secular" government (including control of the lawless and of revolutionaries against the Roman state) they left to others.

While the real reasons for accommodation may have been necessity (making the best of a bad situation) or personal gain (in the case of some members of the *sunedrion*), it was possible to give it a theological justification as well. Thus Paul, as a Roman citizen and perhaps as one influenced by his Pharisaic background, argues that "governing authorities" were instituted by God and continue to exist by the divine will. Thus, one ought to obey their laws and pay one's taxes to them. To do otherwise is to resist the will of God (Romans 13).

It is hardly surprising, then, that Jesus confines his ethical concerns to in-group attitudes and activities, as the "sons of God" await the culmination of the kingdom of God which is even now beginning to manifest itself. What to do with criminals, be they religious or secular, is hardly his concern. The power to deal with them resides with the *bet-din* or has been surrendered to the Romans. Those judiciaries do, in fact, deal with criminals, and both of them are sanctioned to do so by Scripture. (At least, the state could find ample precedent in the Davidic monarchy, which claimed divine sanction for its existence.) Jesus' circumstance and agenda may perhaps be compared with that of the "quad preachers" who appear from time to time on the university campus. They appear without invitation, gather a crowd by their excited rhetoric and overt appeal to hear, and exhort the resultant crowd (complete with hecklers) to live a strict religious life amidst the temptations of their environment. They warn of drink, sex, and drugs, while urging prayer, worship, and charity. They do not deal with the civil and criminal codes of the state, which (as I'm sure the local district attorney would be happy to point out to them) are none of their concern.

There is possibly an additional circumstantial factor which contributed to a lack of teaching concerning capital punishment. During the trial of Jesus, his accusers remind the Roman procurator that "it is not lawful for us to put any man to death" (John 18:31), and there is a late rabbinic tradition to this effect (Babylonian Talmud, *Shabbat* 15a; *Sanhedrin* 41a; Jerusalem Talmud, *Sanhedrin* I.1). Nonetheless, a number of persons were put to death. Is John in error? Were the various killings not legal executions? Does John mean that Jesus is charged with a political crime, and thus falls outside the jurisdiction of his accusers? No certain answer is possible, although the last option seems most likely. If, however, John's statement is taken at face value (all execution is to be sanctioned by the Roman official), then it is interesting that there is no protest against this policy in the pages of the New Testament. The policy would touch at the heart of obedience to *torah:* The blackest crimes could not be punished by those who were commanded to do so. All right to execute would have been surrendered to the state, perhaps with some such theological justification as was offered by Paul (Rom. 13). Jesus, then, would all the more have nothing to say on the matter. As a rabbi of Pharisaic leanings on the matter of response to Rome, he will have given assent to the theological position that "the secular power" may condemn to death those within its realm who violate certain of its laws.

Romans 12:14-19

Paul's advice to "all God's beloved in Rome" might also appear to address our topic: "Bless those who persecute you; bless and do not curse them. . . . Repay no one evil for evil. . . . never avenge yourselves, but leave it to the wrath of God; for it is written, 'Vengeance is mine, I will repay, says the Lord' " (Rom. 12:14-19). Those who would use this perspective to address the issue of capital punishment might well bear the following considerations in mind.

1. The quotation written in this scripture is from Deuteronomy 32:35 (see also Lev. 19:18). Since both Deuteronomy and Leviticus openly and repeatedly sanction execution, God's statement that "vengeance is mine" was in no wise understood by the teachers of ancient Israel to bear on the matter (to say nothing of contradicting the sanction to execute).

2. The context of the quote from Deuteronomy is a review of Israel's history from the point of view of relationship with God (32:7). Despite God's graciousness (vv. 8-14), Israel rebelled (vv. 15-18) and incurred divine displeasure in the form of enemies from without (vv. 19-25). But then God decided to relent, in view of the wickedness of those who had been called to act as instruments against Israel (vv. 26-34). Israel needed to do nothing at this point, since "vengeance is mine . . . and their doom comes swiftly" (v. 35). The basic assertion is that God will act against the foreign nation. It has

nothing to do with individual ethics, and least of all to do with the issue of execution.

3. Paul quotes this text as part of a general exhortation concerning the daily life of the Christian (Rom. 12:1–13:14). How are they to act when they are mistreated, apparently by their fellow Christians (Käsemann, p. 349)? They are not to take justice into their own hands, as if they had legitimate power to act. Sovereignty (RSV, "vengeance") has not been delegated to them, but rightly belongs to God. (On "vengeance" as a mistranslation, see Mendenhall.)

This does not touch upon the matter of whether redress of legitimate grievance should be sought, as a last resort, in the courts. (Note Paul's recognition of limitations: "If possible, so far as it depends upon you," at v. 18.) Courts have been established by divine authority and are sanctioned throughout Scripture (the Pentateuch). Nor does it touch upon the matter of appeal to the Roman courts, which in fact Paul himself does (Acts 25:8-12). Generally, however, he advises that disputes be solved inside the community (I Cor. 6:1-7). It would be astonishing to suppose that Paul, were he rejecting what Scripture has ordained for Israel, would appeal to Scripture as a basis for doing so (note his citation of Deuteronomy).

Least of all does his advice touch upon the duties of those who administer *torah* through established judiciaries. That Christians ought, "so far as depends upon you, [to] live peaceably with all" (v. 18) is one thing; it is quite another to decide what those in positions of authority (be they Christians or not) should do with those who are a danger to individuals or to society as a whole, in violation of the values of God and humanity.

"Redemption and Reconciliation"

Item 10 of a policy statement of the National Council of the Churches of Christ in the United States of America, entitled "Abolition of the Death Penalty," opposes capital punishment because of "our Christian commitment to seek the redemption and reconciliation of the wrong-doer, *which are frustrated by his execution*" (emphasis mine).

The policy statement consists only of brief items with no supporting rationale and thus evaluation of it becomes precarious. What is meant by "reconciliation"? Is it the murderer and the family of the victim? Society at large? The Deity? Does it mean that the murderer comes to realize that such activity is inappropriate? That the murderer is safe to reenter society? That the murderer has a "saving" religious experience? Not all such goals would necessarily be "frustrated" by execution, although the time in which to accomplish them would be shortened.

While it is true that redemption and reconciliation are major themes in the Bible, its near-total emphasis is upon the reconciliation of humans to God as the result of divine initiative (Blackman). It is God alone who can assume the role of redeemer. Nowhere does the Bible itself sense a tension between those processes and its uniform desire that a murderer not be allowed to live. Thus, either the Deity's desires are at cross-purposes with the Bible, or part of the Bible is an outmoded human opinion, or the framers of the policy statement have misunderstood the Bible and created a tension which they then resolved in accordance with their preference. It is doubtful if anyone would opt for the first of these three possibilities. As for the second option, it is but another manifestation of the belief that the Hebrew Bible ("Old" Testament) is not fully Scripture and has been replaced by the New Testament (see chapter 5). This option also fails to realize that the relevant New Testament texts, when studied in their context, do not depart from the perspective of the Hebrew Bible.

CHAPTER X

"The Mind of Christ Jesus"

Some contemporary theologians, uneasy about the use of proof-texts to support capital punishment, propose a more comprehensive beginning point for the discussion: "It is not what the Bible says in a specific verse, but what it says to us through its total message, interpreted in terms of our own conditions, that is relevant" (Milligan, pp. 117-78).

Although this is defensible advice of long standing, it is not without its problems. For example, what if one speaks of verses, rather than of "a specific verse"? Or of various biblical writers who agree with each other? Is there always, on every topic, an undeniable "total message"? If the biblical witness is divided (as it sometimes is), how many verses or perspectives can be ignored? It could be (and indeed has been) argued that some "minority" positions in the Bible are closer to our present context than "majority" ones.

In any case, where might this approach lead one in search of the Bible's "total message" as regards capital punishment? Often it is to the conclusion that we must "strive for that mind which was in Christ Jesus . . . to find the ways and means to love God with our whole being and our neighbor as ourselves" (Milligan, p. 177).

However admirable that may be, it should be noticed that

the entire New Testament constitutes approximately 20 percent of Scripture, and that its reports of Jesus' words and deeds comprise but a fraction of that. Jesus' mind, on a specific topic, or as a whole, can hardly be proposed to be the "total message" of the Bible.

Furthermore, how is one to know "that mind" apart from the careful study of specific biblical accounts of what Jesus said and did? How is one to guard against the natural tendency of modern readers to identify their own minds with that of Jesus? In the previous chapter, I sought to assemble just such necessary information on our topic: Jesus' acceptance of God's unchanging *torah* (Matt. 5:17-19), a *torah* wherein God's unambiguous attitude toward murder is beyond debate; Jesus' repeated encouragement of others to obey the guidelines of *torah* (Matt. 8:1-4; 23:1-3), especially if they would enter eternal life (Matt. 19:16-17); and Jesus' quotation from *torah* specifically about the death penalty (Matt. 15:4). It should not be overlooked, in seeking to discover "the mind of Christ Jesus" on the issue of murder and its punishment, that he goes beyond *torah* to the statement that even verbal abuse makes one deserving of "the hell of fire" (Matt. 5:21-22).

If one seeks to go beyond even these *New Testament* proof-texts, then presumably one would need to deal with such advice as "Judge not," "Neither do I condemn you," and "Love your enemies." Does this suggest that Jesus' mind contradicts his mouth (sayings)? Is this not also a form of proof-texting? In any case, such general advice and approaches to life in the Christian community have been examined above and found wanting (chapter 9, "Some Misused Texts").

In seeking for "the mind of Christ Jesus," modern theologians are often highly selective in the materials which they regard as an indication of that mind. Such texts as the following are likely to be ruled out-of-court, since they may not "fit" a preconceived mold: physically beating those with whom he disagreed (John 2:13-15); berating those religious leaders who disagreed with him by calling them children "of hell" (Matt. 23:15) who deserve to be sentenced to that place (Matt. 23:29-33); designated the Jews (of which he was a part) carte blanche as children of "the devil" (John 8:44); announcing that any place which will not receive his disciples will fare worse than Sodom and Gomorrah (Matt. 10:14-15); responding to a mother's plea for her sick child by telling her that "it is not right to take the children's bread and throw it to the dogs" (i.e., to foreigners; Mark 7:24-27); constantly berating his disciples (e.g., Mark 8:17-18), and even those in need of his help (Mark 9:19); et cetera.

All such possible aberrations in the mind of Jesus to the contrary, what is that mind as it relates to capital punishment? It can be deduced, we are told, by "not approaching these issues by asking what this or that verse says, but by bringing an enlighted and compassionate conscience to the issues. . . . the Christian asks: What can be done, if anything, to redeem this man and to restore his maimed or brutalized humanity?" (Milligan, pp. 177, 180).

While it is certainly allowable for a Christian to bring such *conscience* to the *issue,* this must not be confused with bringing a careful and devoted *study* to the *Bible,* or with acting in accordance with the Bible's agenda. Unfortunately, nowhere does the Bible even hint at one's obligation to restore a murderer's "maimed and brutalized humanity." The very concept (explanation) runs counter to the total message of the Bible: Scripture does not attribute a murderer's status to societal factors, but rather to a deliberate act of rebellion against God.

What may be said by way of summary about "the mind of Christ Jesus" and the issue of capital punishment? (1) There is no way to discover Jesus' "mind" apart from careful study of the reports of his sayings and actions. (2) There is no tension between the teachings of *torah* on capital punishment and the teachings of Jesus on love and forgiveness, when the latter texts are considered in their societal and literary contexts. Modern assertions to the contrary tell us more about the minds of the interpreters than they do about the mind of Jesus.

CHAPTER XI

Summary, Conclusion, Queries, and Observations

*T*he stated goal of the present volume, to describe the biblical practice and mentality as they relate to capital punishment, has now been completed. For the modern Synagogue and Church, however, such a descriptive task cannot be the end of the matter. There remains the even more perplexing isue of what that practice and mentality imply for the faithful in the present. If the Bible is acknowledged to be canon (Scripture), then one must ask not only what it *said* but also what it *says* (means for the present). This necessary task will not lead to uniform results (conclusions), given multiple post-biblical sources of authority to which one may also appeal (e.g., the Talmud and the Fathers of the church). Nonetheless, it may be appropriate, after a summary and statement of conclusion, to raise some queries about what the Bible might or might not say.

Summary

1. Capital punishment was practiced both in ancient Israel (as reflected in the Hebrew Bible) and in Judea in the first century (as reflected in the New Testament).

2. Execution was given theological justification, explicitly in the Hebrew Bible and implicitly in the New Testament.

3. The Pentateuchal rationale for the penalty was not basically in terms of societal order, and thus modern utilitarian values (e.g., does it deter?) have no bearing on the validity of the biblical attitude toward the topic.

4. The motive for the penalty was not a human desire for vengeance (retribution), and thus it cannot justly be criticized by modern theological abolitionists on that basis. (The common word "vengeance," in the English Bible, may be a mistranslation of "sovereignty.")

5. Murder is singled out as among the most serious of capital crimes. Indeed, it is uniquely regarded as an attack upon God.

6. There are no texts in either Testament which overtly depart from the Bible's consensus on this topic.

7. There are no theological stances in either Testament (be they forgiveness of enemies, love, non-vengeance, etc.) which may be taken as an implicit challenge to the consensus.

8. The Bible distinguishes killing in battle, or in self-defense, or in an accident, or as execution, from murder and negligent homicide (which alone merit execution).

Conclusion

For those who desire to bring a theological perspective to the contemporary debate about capital punishment for murder, there is a large amount of biblical data (both descriptive and legislative) to which one may turn for information or guidance. That evidence uniformly authorizes the penalty of death for murder in Israel, throughout the period of the Bible, but it is within the context of the certainty of guilt and of equality before the law. No evidence to the contrary can be found when the texts are studied carefully, contrary to much writing by modern theologians and to proclamations by ecclesiastical structures. Nonetheless, those who would make a direct transfer from *then* to *now*, from what the Bible *said* to what it *says* concerning this topic, are faced with great difficulties. Among the issues to be pondered are the following. To suggest resolution is beyond the scope of the present volume. (On the more general problem of Bible and modern ethics, see the article by Gustafson.)

Queries and Observations

1. Israel's canonical regulations concerning execution were formulated within and for a theocratic society. That is, norms for behavior and sanctions in case of violation were understood to derive from the divine will, and there was no distinction between church and state. Every Israelite, as a party to the covenant by birth, was expected to obey the norms and to understand the appropriateness of the sanctions. Thus, Moses' guidelines are specifically and exclusively addressed to "the people of Israel" (e.g., Exod. 20:22). Nonetheless, all residents within the theocratic state (including resident aliens) were expected to abide by certain of the guidelines (Exod. 12:49) and were to be treated as one would treat a member of the community (Lev. 19:33-34).

Citizens of the United States, by contrast, live in a secular society. Although they may recite (in the "Pledge of Allegiance") a belief in "one nation, under God," it is a perspective with no legal consequence or definition of "God." Nor is the proclaimed "liberty and justice for all" defined by reference to the Bible. Indeed, the Constitution does not even mention God, and it forbids any "establishment of religion." Consequently, many of the capital offenses of the Bible are not crimes in our society and some of them are not even frowned upon by society at large. So far is our self-image of being a "religious" nation from reality that (according to a national survey about a decade ago) scarcely a majority of those who identified themselves as "born-again Christians" could name the four Gospels!

In view of the pluralism of our society, guaranteed by the

Constitution, should those who would take the Bible seriously seek to impose its norms by force upon the whole? In particular, should they seek biblical sanctions (including execution) against those who never accepted the Bible's covenant relationship in the first place? Is the authority of Genesis 9, prior to the Sinai covenant in the storyline and which singles out murder as the crime *par excellence,* of a higher order?

2. Our society, in contrast to that of ancient Israel, makes a distinction between church and state. Only the latter can legally execute a murderer, and it does so for non-biblical reasons. Furthermore, the executioner is an agent of the state and not of the church. Should the religious community nonetheless support the state in this matter, with the justification that "the state's motive and goal may be non-biblical, but the end result is the same"? If so, could such support also be given for execution in case of theft or arson, which were once capital crimes (but are not in the Bible)?

3. Should the modern church abandon the predominant justification for execution (articulated in the Pentateuch), and yet maintain a secondary one (evident in Israel's monarchical history, but best articulated by Paul)? That is, should it make an analogy between the Roman governance of Judea and that of our own time and proclaim the modern state "instituted by God . . . [it] is God's servant for your good . . . to execute his wrath on the wrongdoer"? (Rom. 13:1-4). This is, in fact, the approach which the church has usually tried to take.

However, was Paul's perspective on this matter intended to be an absolute one, so that appeal may be justifiably made to it in the present? In other words, did Paul believe that, at all times and places, the followers of Jesus should obey the laws of their state and subject themselves to its judgments as if they were the judgments of God? Unfortunately, those who would pursue this line of thought must reckon with the conflict between the demands of the gospel and those of tyrannical governments around the world, for example, those of the Nazis. Recently the Reverend Billy Graham quoted this text from Paul to a group of Christians in the Soviet Union, and then realizing the consequences of what he had said, tried desperately to compromise his advice.

By contrast with Paul, note that the prophet Samuel ardently warned the people in ancient Israel concerning the dangers of unbridled kingship at the very inception of that institution (I Sam. 8:10-18). The prophets thundered against monarchical excesses and threatened the kings with divine sanction (I Kings 21:17-20; Amos 7:10-17), even occasionally arranging for succession in a way that bordered on assassination (I Kings 19:15-17; II Kings 8:7-15; 9:1-10). The Wisdom of Solomon (a Deuterocanonical, or Apocryphal, book) warned rulers who "did not rule rightly" that God's judgment would come upon them "terribly and swiftly" (6:4-5).

It is also important to realize that Romans is a pastoral letter to Christians there, and thus (unlike legislative sections of the Hebrew Bible) has no intention of being timeless advice. It was written around 55–57 C.E., early during the reign of Nero, prior to the great persecutions of the church. There was thus some reason for optimism and trust in the Romans under divine sovereignty, in a way that later would be much more difficult (compare the book of Revelation).

It may be argued that Paul's concern was not so much the relationship of Christians in Rome to the state in general as it was what they should do about a specific issue: payment of taxes. Note that the section 13:1-7 ends on precisely that note, as if it were the point toward which the author had been building (Furnish, pp. 117-39). This may have been a troublesome issue (cf. Matt. 22:15-22) which had come to his attention and to which he addressed a specific answer.

It may be doubted, then, that Paul's advice to the Romans is "an apostolic decree for all mankind and all ages . . . making absolute obedience to political authorities part of the central content of his message" (in agreement with Käsemann, p. 355; contrast Ryrie, p. 214).

4. Israel's willingness to take a human life presupposed certainty as to guilt. Thus, in case of murder, testimony of two eyewitnesses was required for conviction. Building upon this foundation, and aware of the frailties of human nature and the power of observation, the rabbis of the Tannaitic period (first to third centuries C.E.) and of the Talmudic period (fourth to fifth centuries C.E.) examined witnesses so minutely that conviction was exceedingly difficult. (For the procedure, with illustrations, see Goldin, pp. 89-130; Mendelsohn, pp. 115-32.)

Whereas biblical and rabbinic courts would not allow circumstantial evidence in the trial of one accused of murder, modern technology has now made it, in some instances, more reliable than eyewitness testimony. Fidelity to the ancient demand for certainty, therefore, might require, for the modern Christian or Jew, some reversal of the kind of evidence that is adequate (eyewitnesses being notoriously fallible). Nonetheless, that fidelity would require certitude, and not merely "guilt beyond a reasonable doubt," since erroneous execution (well documented in our society—Bedau, pp. 434-52; McNamara, p. 187) is beyond remedy.

Should one sanction execution on biblical grounds, without concern (indeed, demand) for its attendant safeguards?

5. It is a fundamental assumption of biblical jurisprudence that the socio-economic status of the accused will have no bearing upon the verdict. The inequities which had been built into the codes of their neighbors (advantages for the powerful and affluent) were well known to those who, under divine inspiration, formulated and edited Israel's sacred literature, and deliberate steps were apparently taken to eliminate them.

While inequity is not necessarily built into our modern judicial codes (tax law being an exception?), it nevertheless has resulted from a number of factors, among them: discretion by judges and district attorneys; illogic, prejudice, and sentiment on the part of jurors; and the setting of attorney fees by free market standards (i.e., the ablest attorneys may charge the highest fees and thus justice may be de facto for sale to the highest bidder). Thus, the inequities of our system, statues of *Blind Justice* on courthouse facades to the contrary, are glaringly evident. One's chances of being convicted, sentenced to die, and actually executed are apparently related to one's sex, race, and income (J. Greenberg; MacNamara, pp. 188-89). Indeed, in 1972 the U.S. Supreme Court ruled that under existing laws execution was so "harsh, freakish, and arbitrary" that it constituted "cruel and unusual punishment in violation of the Eighth and Fourteenth Amendments" (*Furman v. Georgia*, 408 U.S. 238). (The opinion of Justice William O. Douglas in this case contained the following statement: "One searches our chronicles in vain for the execution of any member of the affluent strata of this society.") State legislatures then enacted new statutes that were designed to meet the Court's objections, and one type (mandatory execution for specified crimes) has subsequently been ruled unconstitutional under the same amendments (*Woodson v. North Carolina*, 428 U.S. 280).

As long as glaring inequities in conviction and sentencing remain in our modern secular society, should conscientious Jews and Christians appeal to the jurists of ancient Israel in support of the death penalty? Should such conscientious persons work for the abolition of the penalty, or for the elimination of the inequity?

In sum: Although there is no biblical basis for objection to the death penalty per se (and indeed there is a mandate to carry it out within an autonomous community whose ultimate authority is the Bible), the divergencies between Israelite society and our own raise very serious questions with which

Church and Synagogue must struggle. It is not automatically to be assumed that the divergencies are sufficient to call for the abolition of the penalty, however. Prior to that conclusion should come the strenuous demand that there be certainty as to guilt (serial murders present a better case, perhaps) and that there be equity before the law.

CHAPTER XII

Quotations from
Post-biblical Sources

*T*he following collection of quotations is by no means illustrative of the full range of opinion in Synagogue and Church. If important testimony is not included, I can only remind the reader that my goal has been to state what the *Bible* says. Nonetheless, the collection does contain statements by revered figures whose opinions are of importance to contemporary members of those two religious communities.

Proper understanding of each quotation would necessitate the kind of background information that I have given for the relevant texts from the Bible. Such information I have neither the training nor the space to supply. Nonetheless, it is interesting to note the basis upon which each statement rests and the language with which it is expressed. Has the speaker understood the Bible? Is the Bible's opinion on this crucial issue accepted as divine revelation, or as time-conditioned human opinion? Is the starting point of the quotation theological, or is it sociological? (About these matters, I make no value judgment, but rather seek only to alert readers who may then evaluate the statements as they will.)

1. Be not righteous overmuch [(Eccles. 7:16). This means] do not be more righteous than your Creator. This [text] refers to Saul . . . who debated with his Creator and said, "God

said, 'Go and smite Amalek' [I Sam. 15:3]. But [even] if the men are guilty, the women and children are yet innocent, and the oxen and donkeys are innocent, too." A voice answered from heaven, "Be not more righteous than your Creator." (*Ecclesiastes Rabbah,* 7.33)

This collection of rabbinic materials, which may have taken its final shape as late as the eighth century c.e., implies that when an action in the Bible seems offensive to interpreters in the present, it cannot be set aside (i.e., denied the status of revelation) on the basis of a proposed higher morality, as if one were superior to Scripture.

2. "Your eye shall not pity him" [Deut. 19:13]. This is an admonition not mercifully to spare the killer. We should not say, "The one has already been killed, [so] of what use is the killing of the other?" Thus the execution would be neglected. Rather, he must be killed. (*Midrash Tannaim,* 115b; see also *Sifre* on Deut. 18:7)

These two Tannaitic (first to third centuries c.e.) commentaries on Deuteronomy address an attitude that is common in our own society, and indeed it must have been present in ancient Israel for Scripture to have spoken as it does. However meritorious mercy may be, and however abundantly evident it may be in God's own dealings with creatures, murder was an offense for which no such response was to be allowed.

3. The Sanhedrin that puts to death one person in seven years is termed tyrannical. . . . Rabbi Tarfon and Rabbi Akiba say, "If we had been in the Sanhedrin, no one would ever have been put to death." Rabban Simon ben Gamaliel says, "They would indeed have [thereby] increased the shedders of blood in Israel." (Mishnah *Makkot* 1.10)

The motives of Tarfon and Akiba have been much discussed (Blidstein, pp. 163-65): recognition of human fallibility in reaching a verdict? Awareness of societal abuse of the penalty? A reluctance to take human life? Although their opinion was not authoritative, and its negative practical consequences are pointed out, nonetheless it marks a growing tendency of the rabbis "toward the complete abolition of the death penalty" (*Encyclopedia Judaica*, vol. 5, p. 147).

4. For when God prohibits killing . . . He warns [us] not to do even those things which are regarded as legal among men. And so it will not be lawful for a just man . . . to accuse anyone of a capital offense . . . since killing itself is forbidden. And so, in this commandment of God, no exception at all ought to be made [to the rule] that it is always wrong to kill a man, whom God has wished to be [regarded as] a sacrosanct creature. (Lactantius, *Divinae Institutiones*, VI.xx.15, as translated in C. J. Cadoux, *The Early Church and the World* [Edinburgh: T. & T. Clark, 1925])

The unclarity of the sixth commandment has led Lactantius (a Christian apologist of the early fourth century) astray, as it has many since his time. He is, however, rightly aware of the excesses to which states may go in imposing the death penalty, especially in view of the persecution of the church. (For inconsistencies in his writings concerning the administration of justice, see Cadoux, p. 547.)

5. The same divine law which forbids the killing of a human being allows certain exceptions, as when God authorizes killing by a general law or when He gives an explicit commission to an individual for a limited time. Since the agent . . . is not responsible for the killing, it is in no way contrary to the commandment, "Thou shalt not kill," to wage war at God's bidding, or for the representatives of the State's authority to put criminals to death, according to law or the rule of rational justice. (Augustine, *The City of God*, book I, chapter 21, at the beginning)

Augustine, a bishop in North Africa, wrote *The City of God* between 412 and 426 C.E. He is often regarded as "the Father of Western Christianity."

6. Now every individual person is as it were a part of the whole. Therefore if any man is dangerous to the community and is subverting it by some sin, the treatment to be commended is his execution in order to preserve the common good. (Thomas Aquinas, *Summa Theologiae,* 2a2ae, 64.2, Reply)

A university professor in Germany, France, and Italy, Aquinas (1225?–1274 C.E.) remains one of the great teachers of the church.

7. Mr. Everybody is no Christian. The king, the princes, and the lords must use the sword and remove heads; capital punishment must continue that the others may be kept in fear, and the pious . . . tend to their work. (Martin Luther, as quoted in *What Luther Says,* ed. Ewald M. Plass, vol. 2 [St. Louis: Concordia, 1959], no. 1781)

This passage [Gen. 9:6] we should carefully note. Here God has established civil authority, to sit in judgment not only on life and death but also on matters of minor importance. (Luther, in Plass, vol. 2, no. 1814)

If a malicious scoundrel wants to . . . beat and stab at provocation of a word, let justice be meted out to him at the place of public execution. (Luther, in Plass, vol. 2, no. 1815)

The passion with which Luther speaks on the topic likely reflects the peasant disturbances at the time.

8. If what we are to attest in the sphere of human punishment is not a self-conceived, imaginary and lifeless justice, but the righteousness of the true God who has acted and revealed Himself in Jesus Christ, capital punishment will surely be the very last thing to enter our heads. (Karl Barth,

Church Dogmatics, vol. 3, part 4 [Edinburgh: T. & T. Clark, 1961], p. 443)

This is an obvious departure from the previously quoted (and correct) understandings of the Bible. It is interesting to note that the modern denial of the state's right to execute its criminals is usually traced back to an essay entitled *Dei delitti e della pene* (1764) by the Italian Cesare Beccaria. He appealed to "enlightened" rulers to realize that execution was "neither necessary nor useful," and has been called "the father of modern penal reform." (See *New Catholic Encyclopedia,* vol. 3, pp. 79-81, "Capital Punishment.")

9. In the love of Christ who came to save those who are lost and vulnerable, we urge the creation of genuinely new systems of rehabilitation that will restore, preserve, and nurture the humanity of the imprisoned. For the same reason, we oppose capital punishment and urge its elimination from all criminal codes. (*Book of Discipline of The United Methodist Church,* par. 74, sec. F, p. 101)

10.　　Because the Christian believes in the inherent worth of human personality and in the unceasing availability of God's mercy, forgiveness, and redemptive power, and

Because the Christian wholeheartedly supports the emphasis in modern penology upon the process of creative, redemptive rehabilitation rather than on punishment and primitive retribution, and

Because the deterrent effects of capital punishment are not supported by available evidence, and

Because the death penalty tends to brutalize the human spirit and the society which condones it, and

Because human agencies of legal justice are fallible, permitting the possibility of the executing of the innocent,

We, therefore, recommend the abolition of capital punishment and the re-evaluation of the parole system relative to such cases.

(Resolution adopted by the American Baptist Convention in 1960, reproduced in Adam Bedau, ed., *The Death Penalty in America* [Garden City, N.Y.: Doubleday and Co., 1964], pp. 167-68)

11. In support of current movements to abolish the death penalty, the National Council of Churches hereby declares its opposition to capital punishment. In so doing, it finds itself in substantial agreement with a number of member denominations which have already expressed opposition to the death penalty.

Reasons for taking this position include the following:

(1) The belief in the worth of human life and the dignity of human personality as gifts of God;

(2) A preference for rehabilitation rather than retribution in the treatment of offenders;

(3) Reluctance to assume the responsibility of arbitrarily terminating the life of a fellow-being solely because there has been a transgression of law;

(4) Serious question that the death penalty serves as a deterrent to crime, evidenced by the fact that the homicide rate has not increased disproportionally in those states where capital punishment has been abolished;

(5) The conviction that institutionalized disregard for the sanctity of human life contributes to the brutalization of society;

(6) The possibility of errors in judgment and the irreversibility of the penalty which makes impossible any restitution to one who has been wrongfully executed;

(7) Evidence that economically poor defendants, particularly members of racial minorities, are more likely to be executed than others because they cannot afford exhaustive legal defenses;

(8) The belief that not only the severity of the penalty but also its increasing infrequency and the ordinarily long delay between sentence and execution subject the condemned person to cruel, unnecessary and unusual punishment;

(9) The belief that the protection of society is served as well by restraint and rehabilitation, and that society may actually benefit from the contribution of the rehabilitated offender;

(10) Our Christian commitment to seek the redemption and reconciliation of the wrong-doer, which are usually frustrated by his execution.

Seventy-five nations of the world and thirteen states of

the United States have abolished the death penalty with no evident detriment to social order. It is our judgment that the remaining jurisdictions should move in the same humane direction.

In view of the foregoing, the National Council of Churches urges abolition of the death penalty under federal and state law in the United States, and urges member denominations and state and local councils of churches actively to promote the necessary legislation to secure this end, particularly in the thirty-seven states which have not yet eliminated capital punishment.

103 FOR   0 AGAINST   0 ABSTENTIONS

(Policy statement of the National Council of the Churches of Christ in the United States of America, "Abolition of the Death Penalty," adopted by the General Board September 13, 1968)

The Bible's Legal Sections

*T*he careful reader of Israel's legal materials will be struck by their diversity in form, language, and content. Some of them will be illustrative cases in the third person, for example, "When (or if) so-and-so happens, then . . . " (Exod. 21:1–22:16). Others are direct orders in the second person, for example, "You shall . . . ; You shall not" (Exod. 22:18–23:19). Some of them announce the death sentence as "shall be put to death" while others use a variety of other expressions. Some of them seem to presuppose settled (and agricultural) life in Canaan (owning slaves, oxen, fields, growing grain: Exod. 21:1-6, 28-32; 22:5-6), while others do not.

Such readers may also be puzzled by the fact that some of the Bible's major characters violate its prohibitions, seemingly with impunity. For example, marriage to one's sister is forbidden by Leviticus 18:9 and 20:17, and yet it is done by Abraham (Gen. 20:12) and allowable at the time of David (II Sam. 13:13). Simultaneous marriage to sisters is forbidden by Leviticus 18:18, and yet forms the core of one of the Bible's famous stories (Gen. 29:15-30). There is to be only one legitimate sanctuary in the land of Canaan (Deut. 12:1-14), namely Jerusalem (Ps. 132:11-18), and one legitimate priesthood (the Levites, according to Deut. 33:8-11), and yet we find the prophet Elijah (not a Levite) erecting an altar and offering sacrifice on Mount Carmel (I Kings 18).

The conscientious reader's mind will be relieved by the knowledge that the conflicting legal materials, in their present form, are not the product of a single mind, time, and place. Rather, the Bible's stories (with legislation embedded), regardless of their age, became authoritative (Scripture) in stages, maintaining their diversity, creating repetitions, and making some of its leading characters appear (retroactively) to be in violation of them.

In the classic reconstruction of the growth of the Pentateuchal literature, there are four stages. Each stage involved the compilation and arrangement of traditional (earlier) materials, as well as creative application to the present and possible supplementation by the compilers. The stages have come to be called:

1. The Yahwistic Literature. The name is derived from the use of the divine name Yahweh in its traditions (English Bible, "the Lord"). It is often given the siglum "J," because of the belief that it originated in Judah, around the beginning of the monarchical period (1000 B.C.E.).

2. The Elohistic Literature. The name is derived from the use of the word "god" (Hebrew: *'elohim*) in its traditions. It is given the siglum "E," because of the possibility that it originated in Ephraim, sometime later in the monarchical period (850–750 B.C.E.?).

3. The Deuteronomic Literature. The name is derived from the fact that it consists of the book of Deuteronomy, and thus it is given the siglum "D." It is dated prior to the time of the reform of King Josiah (621 B.C.E.).

4. The Priestly Literature. The name is derived from its cultic concerns. It is thus given the siglum "P," and is dated to the exilic and early post-exilic periods (550–450 B.C.E.).

The reasons for this classic reconstruction (sometimes called "The Documentary Hypothesis"), as well as a discussion of the major options, may be found in Bailey, *The Pentateuch,* chapter 1.

The major sections of the Pentateuchal law are as follows.

1. The Ten Commandments (Exod. 20:2-17; Deut. 5:6-21) and the related "cultic (or ritual) decalogue" (Exod. 34:14-26).

2. The Book of the Covenant (Exod. 20:23–23:19), which takes its name from Exodus 24:7.

3. The Deuteronomic Legislation (chapters 12-26).

4. The Priestly Legislation (Lev. 1–27, as well as sections of Num. 1–10). Chapters 17–26, called the Holiness Code, are sometimes considered separately.

It is common to relate these legal materials to the aforementioned four stages of compilation of Pentateuchal materials as follows:

J: The "cultic decalogue" of Exodus 34, which is sometimes called the "Yahwistic decalogue."

E: The Ten Commandments as expressed in Exodus 20, sometimes called the "Elohistic decalogue." (There are difficulties with this source assignment, however.)

D: The Ten Commandments as expressed in Deuteronomy 5, as well as chapters 12–26.

P: The Priestly Legislation.

This leaves aside the Book of the Covenant, which seems to have an independent origin, but belongs to the J and E periods.

One may thus understand the acceptability of the account of Abraham's marriage to a sister (Gen. 20:12, source E), since the feeling that this was improper did not have the force of Scripture until the sixth to fifth centuries B.C.E. (Lev. 18:9, source P).

For a helpful discussion of how to study the Pentateuchal laws, as well as an up-to-date presentation of the background of each section, see Patrick, *Old Testament Law.*

The Meaning of *Môt Yûmat*

Ordinarily in the Hebrew Bible, articulation of a capital offense is concluded by the phrase *môt yûmat*, usually translated into English as "he shall be put to death." The element *môt* is an infinitive (of the verb *m-w-t*, "to die"), while *yûmat* is the so-called "imperfect" conjugation (ordinarily the equivalent of the future tense in English), third masculine singular, of the same verb. (The infinitive serves to express emphasis, corresponding to the English word "surely" or "indeed.")

Such a phrase, devoid of a literary context, is ambiguous as to its grammatical mood. That is, the Hebrew language, by the time of its present biblical form, has ceased to express formally what we would call "modal auxiliaries." Thus, is the phrase indicative (declarative, a statement of fact): "he *will* be"? Is the phrase subjunctive (a demand): "(I, God, demand *that*) he *be,*" which is better expressed as "he *shall* be"? Does it express a wish: "he *should* be"? Does it express permission or allow an option: "he *may* be"?

A few writers have opted for the last of these possibilities. Thus Buss (p. 56) remarks: "It is far from certain that the threat is regularly carried out; the phrase *mōt yūmat* (which can be translated, 'he may be killed') does not command an execution." However, he can find no clear example where such optional leniency was exercised. He cites Ezekiel 23:25 for "mutilation as a possible penalty" for adultery instead of execution (along with the "wide latitude enjoyed by the husband in [the Mesopotamian code of the city of] Eshnunna"). Note, however, that the prophet discusses the apostasy of Israel and Judah with the Babylonians by means of an analogy with two spouses who have turned to harlotry. In punishment the Deity will "rouse against you your lovers . . . the Babylonians. . . . they shall come against you. . . . They shall cut off your nose and your ears" (23:22, 23, 24, 25b). It is the Babylonians, then, in accordance with their own customs, who exact this penalty, and thus the text has no bearing on Israel's penal system. That is, Ezekiel 23:25 does not support Buss' understanding of the phrase *môt yûmat*.

The phrase is rendered in standard English translation in the following ways at Exodus 21:12: "Whoever strikes a man so that he dies

  . . . shall be put to death" (RSV, NEB).

  . . . must be put to death" (NAB, NJB).

  . . . shall surely be put to death" (NIV; compare, KJV, NASB).

  . . . is to be put to death" (TEV).

  . . . must die" (JB).

The Trials of Jesus and His Followers

*P*erhaps, with the previous background, the capital charge and the jurisdiction of famous trials in the New Testament will become clear.

1. The trials of Peter and John (Acts 4:1-22; 5:17-41). Note that the arresting officials are priests and Sadducees (4:1); rulers, elders, scribes, and High Priest (4:5-6); Sadducees and High Priest (5:21). Peter and John are brought before the "council" *(sunedrion)* and "senate" *(gerousia).* These factors suggest that the charges were political, although the disciples' recorded response is in the sphere of religion. Their accusers were "annoyed because they were teaching the people and proclaiming in Jesus the resurrection from the dead" (4:2), but this is not a violation of *torah* which should lead to trial by the (religious) *bet-din.* The accusers are further concerned that the movement with which the disciples are associated "spread no further among the people" (4:17), and they are worried that "they intend to bring this man's [i.e., Jesus'] blood upon us" (5:28). Such popular unrest should not reach the ears of their Roman overlords, especially since these two men are speaking in the name of "Jesus Christ of Nazareth, whom you crucified" (4:10). That crucifixion centered upon the political charge that he was "King of the Jews" (Matt. 27:37), and hence a challenge to Roman authority. Apparently with the fear of potential rebellion in mind, a member of the *sunedrion* made an analogy with two previous rebels who incited violence and caused slaughter by the Romans (5:34-39).

2. *The trial of Stephen (Acts 6:8–7:60)*. The charge is that he had blasphemed against "Moses and God," with the accusers being members of various synagogues (Acts 6:9). Both the charge and the accusers suggest a religious offense, which would have mandated trial by the "small" *bet-din*. Apparently here it is called, anachronistically, a *sunedrion*. (This is understandable in view of the date of the book of Acts: after the destruction of the Temple, following which the terms *bet-din* and *sunedrion* become identified.) Note that there is no mention of the High Priest, whose presence would have been necessary to call a political council *(sunedrion)* into session.

In his speech (7:2-53), Stephen does not use the divine name, so that a charge of blasphemy against the Holy Name (Lev. 24:16, clarified by Mishnah *Sanhedrin* 7.5) could only come from (false?) witnesses. By "blasphemy against Moses" they may have meant that he had taught that *torah* was not of eternal significance (6:14). In any case, it is not clear that the court found him guilty, and some interpreters have suggested that he was, in effect, set upon by an enraged mob.

3. *The attack upon Paul (Acts 21:26-32)*. The ground plan for the Temple of New Testament times (the Herodian Temple) provided for a Court of Gentiles, beyond which they could not go on penalty of death. (The original inscription, warning to this effect, has been unearthed.) Violators, such as Paul was accused of being, were subject to attack and execution without warning or trial. This may be comparable with the warning against trespass upon sacred area in Exodus 19:12-13.

4. *Paul's various trials (Acts 22:30–23:10; 24:1-23; 25:1-12; 26:1-32)*. That the perceived danger from this man lay in the political sphere is clear from the fact that a Roman officer ordered the High Priest and the *sunedrion* to hear the case

(22:30), from the fact that part of the council consisted of Sadducees (23:6; they did not even recognize the validity of the *bet-din* and hence never were members of it), from the fact that the case was referred to the Roman governor (23:24), from the fact that he was accused of being "a pestilent fellow, an agitator" (24:5), and from the fact that Paul appealed to Caesar for trial as a Roman citizen (25:12). Paul's fate was execution by beheading (so the early Christian authorities Origen, Tertullian, and Eusebius). He must, then, have been adjudged a danger to the state.

5. *The trial of Jesus (Matt. 26:47–27:50; Mark 14:43–15:37; Luke 22:47–23:46; John 18:1–19:30).* With the nature of the other trials in memory, the nature of the charges against Jesus should now be clear. He was arrested by Roman soldiers and officials of the High Priest (John 18:3), brought before the High Priest (Matt. 26:57), examined by a *sunedrion* (Matt. 26:59), asked specifically if he claimed to be the Messiah (Matt. 26:63), examined by the Roman governor (Matt. 27:1-2), condemned for fear that he would precipitate a bloodbath at the hands of the Roman soldiers (John 11:47-50), specifically charged with being "King of the Jews" (Matt. 27:31), executed with two brigands (Matt. 27:38; persons of similar danger to the state?), and had his clothing confiscated (Mark 15:24, which was done only to political prisoners).

It is plausible to conclude, then, that Jesus was crucified by the Romans and their local quislings (in the *sunedrion*) on political grounds, rather than by the respected religious leaders (the Pharisaic *bet-din*) on religious grounds. The revelance of this conclusion, from the point of view of the present volume, is this: Roman authority in civil matters (including execution) was recognized, not merely by the religious leadership of Judah, but also by Jesus (Matt. 22:15-22) and Paul (Rom. 13:1-7), the latter giving it a theological underpinning. Rome's right to execute Jesus, therefore, was never questioned.

Homicide as the Context of the Flood Narrative

T he Genesis account states that the Lord decided to destroy humanity because "the wickedness of man was great in the earth" (6:5) and because "the earth was filled with violence" (6:11). No specifics concerning the wickedness and violence are provided in the flood story itself, which runs from 6:5 to 8:22. It is clear, however, that the concern is not an innate sinfulness of human beings, as if one were reading a timeless observation of human nature. Rather, a situational observation of events has led to a crisis.

It is plausible to suggest that the nature of the crisis may be clarified by the larger context. That is, the account of the great deluge, a self-contained story which could be told on its own, has been placed at a certain point within the bounds of the primeval events of Genesis 1–11. Unless such an editorial placement was unreflective, then the stories immediately before and after the flood account may indicate the nature of the "wickedness" and the "violence." It would be especially significant if the preceding material presented instances of a problem which the succeeding material then sought to remedy. Such, apparently, is the case.

Since it is the succeeding material that is the more focused, let us begin at that point. God's relationship to and expectations of a purged and renewed humanity are stated in

9:1-17 (see also 8:20-22) and have four aspects, consisting of three commandments and a promise: (1) to flourish upon the earth ("be fruitful and multiply"); (2) restrictions upon the consumption of meat ("only you shall not eat . . . its blood"); (3) human life is sacred to the Deity, so that homicide results in the ultimate penalty ("by man shall his blood be shed"); and (4) God now gives unconditional approval to the continuation of creation ("never again shall all flesh be cut off").

It is clear, then, that two practices are not to be tolerated: the consumption of blood and the taking of human life with impunity. Are these in fact depicted as pre-flood practices? The prior diet of humans had been specified at Genesis 1:29-30: "Every plant . . . fruit . . . you shall have them for food." After the flood, this is expanded to include meat, but with the aforementioned restriction. Whether the text suggests that humans have, in the meanwhile, exceeded their mandate and become carnivorous is a moot point.

Prior human excesses in the other area, however, are well attested in the biblical text. They begin with Cain's murder of his brother, an act for which the Deity shields him from retribution (4:1-16). The reasons why this cannot serve as an anti-execution precedent have been given above in chapter 3. Thereafter we read that Lamech, having "slain a man for wounding me," claims an immunity far exceeding that of his ancestor: "If Cain is avenged sevenfold, truly Lamech seventy-sevenfold" (4:23-24). It is now a matter of boastful arrogance for which there was no divine sanction, save perhaps in Lamech's imagination. It is indeed an indication of a dangerous situation, one that could well lead to an earth "filled with violence" (6:11) and necessitate both the cleansing flood and subsequent restrictions (9:5-6).

This contextual (holistic) reading of the flood story, with its indications of murder as the prime offense, has an apparent parallel in one version of the Mesopotamian deluge account (so Frymer-Kensky). In the Atrahasis Epic, the flood story is also set in the context of primeval events, beginning with the creation of humans. Soon thereafter, overpopulation (a historical reality in the narrow valleys of the Tigris and Euphrates where this version of the flood story had its origin) led to disturbance of the creator-gods' sleep and steps were taken (drought, plague, saline soil), unsuccessfully, to reduce human numbers. Finally, the ultimate remedy is proposed and enacted: a devastating flood. (One family, that of Atrahasis, survives the deluge in a boat and then begins the process of repopulation.) However, the concern which led to the flood is now resumed: More effective and long-term methods of population control are instituted (sterility, stillbirth, and celibacy). These regulations would seem to be the functional equivalents of the commandments given to Noah in Genesis 9, which thus suggests the motive for the flood in the first place.

In each case, the flood results from a perceived intolerable encroachment upon divine realities: In Mesopotamia it is overpopulation; in Israel it arguably is murder. Thus, murder is not only an attack upon God (see above, chapter 2), but apparently the most serious of offenses which so pollutes the land that the Deity cannot "dwell" in it until it is cleansed by the waters of the deluge. Thereafter, this evil tendency of humans is addressed by divine sanction for execution.

Bailey, Lloyd. *Biblical Perspectives on Death.* Philadelphia: Fortress Press, 1979.

———. *The Pentateuch.* Nashville: Abingdon Press, 1981.

Bedau, Hugo A. "Murder, Errors of Justice, and Capital Punishment." In *The Death Penalty in America,* edited by Hugo A. Bedau, pp. 434-52. Garden City, N.Y.: Doubleday and Co., 1964. 3rd edition, 1982.

Blackman, E. C. "Reconciliation, Reconcile." In *The Interpreter's Dictionary of the Bible,* edited by George Buttrick et al., vol. 4, pp. 16-17. Nashville: Abingdon Press, 1962.

Blidstein, Gerald J. "Capital Punishment—The Classic Jewish Discussion." *Judaism* 14 (Spring 1965), pp. 159-71.

Boecker, Hans Jochen. *Law and the Administration of Justice in the Old Testament and Ancient Near East.* Minneapolis: Augsburg Publishing House, 1980.

Brown, Raymond E. *The Gospel According to John (I-XII).* The Anchor Bible, vol. 29. Garden City, N.Y.: Doubleday and Co., 1966.

Buss, Martin J. "The Distinction between Civil and Criminal Law in Ancient Israel." In *Sixth World Congress of Jewish Studies,* vol. 1, pp. 51-62. Jerusalem: Academic Press, 1977.

Cadoux, Cecil John. *The Early Church and the World.* Edinburgh: T. & T. Clark, 1925.

Childs, Brevard. *The Book of Exodus.* Old Testament Library. Philadelphia: Westminster Press, 1974.

DeWolf, L. Harold. "The Death Penalty: Cruel, Unusual, Unethical, and Futile." *Religion in Life* 42 (1973), pp. 37-41.

Frymer, T. S. "Ordeal, Judicial." In *The Interpreter's Dictionary of the Bible, Supplementary Volume,* edited by Keith Crim et al., pp. 638-40. Nashville: Abingdon Press, 1976.

Frymer-Kensky, Tikva. "The Atrahasis Epic and Its Significance for Our Understanding of Genesis 1–9." *Biblical Archaeologist* 40 (1977), pp. 147-55.

Furnish, Victor Paul. *The Moral Teaching of Paul.* Nashville: Abingdon Press, 1979. Chapter 5 is entitled "Christians and the Governing Authorities."

Gaster, Theodor H. *Myth, Legend, and Custom in the Old Testament.* New York: Harper & Row, 1969.

Goldin, Hyman E. *Hebrew Criminal Law and Procedure, Mishnah: Sanhedrin-Makkot.* New York: Twayne Publishers, 1952.

Good, Edwin M. "Capital Punishment and Its Alternatives in Ancient Near Eastern Law." *Stanford Law Review* 19 (May 1967), pp. 947-77.

Greenberg, Jack. "Against the American System of Capital Punishment." *Harvard Law Review* 99 (1986), pp. 1670-80.

Greenberg, Moshe. "Crimes and Punishments." In *The Interpreter's Dictionary of the Bible,* edited by George Buttrick et al., vol. 1, pp. 733-44. Nashville: Abingdon Press, 1962. An excellent introductory survey.

Gustafson, James M. "The Place of Scripture in Christian Ethics: A Methodological Study." *Interpretation* 24 (1970), pp. 430-55.

Harrelson, Walter. *The Ten Commandments and Human Rights.* Philadelphia: Fortress Press, 1980. A helpful discussion of ancient meaning and contemporary implications.

Holladay, W. L. "Grace in the OT." In *The Interpreter's Dictionary of the Bible, Supplementary Volume,* edited by Keith Crim et al., pp. 375-77. Nashville: Abingdon Press, 1976. A strong antidote to the position that there is a contrast between the two Testaments as regards God's judgment and graciousness.

Käsemann, Ernst. *Commentary on Romans.* Grand Rapids: Wm. B. Eerdmans Pub. Co., 1980.

Lillie, W. "Towards a Biblical Doctrine of Punishment." *Scottish Journal of Theology* 21 (1968), pp. 449-61.

MacNamara, Donald E. J. "Statement against Capital Punishment." In *The Death Penalty in America,* edited by Hugo A. Bedau, pp. 182-94. Garden City, N.Y.: Doubleday and Co., 1984.

Megivern, James J. "Biblical Arguments in the Capital Punishment Debate." *Perspectives in Religious Studies* 8 (1981), pp. 143-53. A brief survey of the debate in the United States, beginning in the 1700s.

Mendelsohn, S. *The Criminal Jurisprudence of the Ancient Hebrews.* 2nd ed. New York: Hermon Press, 1968.

Mendenhall, George. *The Tenth Generation: The Origins of the Biblical Tradition.* Baltimore: Johns Hopkins University Press, 1973. In chapter 3 ("The 'Vengeance' of Yahweh") he argues strenuously that the Hebrew verb *n-q-m* has erroneously been translated "to take vengeance," thus subjecting the Hebrew Bible to groundless criticism. Rather, the verb denotes "the legitimate power to act." Thus, the religious community, in executing a murderer, does not exercise "vengeance" or self-help, but exercises the executive authority of God which has been delegated to it.

Milligan, Charles S. "A Protestant's View of the Death Penalty." In *The Death Penalty in America*, edited by Hugo A. Bedau, pp. 175-82. Garden City, N.Y.: Doubleday and Co., 1964. This essay is part of chapter 4, "The Argument Against the Death Penalty."

Nahamani, H. S. *Human Rights in the Old Testament*. Tel Aviv: J. Chachik Publishing House, 1964.

Patrick, Dale. *Old Testament Law*. Atlanta: John Knox Press, 1985. A helpful introduction to the individual legal sections of the Hebrew Bible.

Phillips, Anthony. *Ancient Israel's Criminal Law*. New York: Schocken Books, 1970.

Priest, J. F. "Etiology." In *The Interpreter's Dictionary of the Bible, Supplementary Volume*, edited by Keith Crim et al., pp. 293-95. Nashville: Abingdon Press, 1976.

Rad, Gerhard von. *Genesis*. The Old Testament Library. Philadelphia: Westminster Press, 1961.

Renger, J. M. "Lex Talionis." In *The Interpreter's Dictionary of the Bible, Supplementary Volume*, edited by Keith Crim et al., pp. 545-46. Nashville: Abingdon Press, 1976.

Rivkin, Ellis. *What Crucified Jesus?* Nashville: Abingdon Press, 1984.

Ryrie, Charles C. "The Doctrine of Capital Punishment." *Bibliotheca Sacra* 129 (July 1972), pp. 211-17.

Sanders, J. A. "Torah." In *The Interpreter's Dictionary of the Bible, Supplementary Volume*, edited by Keith Crim et al., pp. 909-11. Nashville: Abingdon Press, 1976. A study of the meaning of the Hebrew word *torah* and of the Greek translation *nomos*, both erroneously rendered into English as "law," giving rise to the supposed contrast between "law" and "gospel."

Vellenga, Jacob J. "Christianity and the Death Penalty." In *The Death Penalty in America*, edited by Hugo A. Bedau, pp. 129-30. Garden City, N.Y.: Doubleday and Co., 1964. This essay is part of chapter 3, "The Argument for the Death Penalty."

Wenham, G. J. *The Book of Leviticus*. Grand Rapids: Wm. B. Eerdmans Pub. Co., 1979. See especially "Excursus I: Principles of Punishment in the Pentateuch," pp. 281-86.

Westerman, Claus. *Genesis 1–11*. Minneapolis: Augsburg Publishing House, 1984. A reliable, up-to-date, and detailed discussion of the relevant texts (e.g., Genesis 9).

Williams, Jay G. *Ten Words of Freedom*. Philadelphia: Fortress Press, 1971.

Zeitlin, Solomon. *Who Crucified Jesus?* New York: Block Publishing Company, 1964.